Historic
Lunenburg

HISTORIC
LUNENBURG

The Days of Sail
1880—1930

M IKE P ARKER

NIMBUS
PUBLISHING

Nimbus Publishing Limited
PO Box 9301, Station A
Halifax, NS   B3K 5N5
(902) 455-4286

Design: Heather Bryan
Printed and bound in Canada

Canadian Cataloguing in Publication Data
Parker, Mike, 1952-
Historic Lunenburg
Includes bibliographic references
ISBN 1-55109-297-2
1. Lunenburg (N.S.) -- History -- Pictorial works. I. Title.
FC2349.L85P37 1999   971.6'23   C99-950214-X
F1039.5.L86P37 1999

Cover photo: Lunenburg waterfront, ca. 1934. See page 19.
Title page: Lunenburg schooner *J.B. Young* and
her crew at dockside. See page 8.

Nimbus Publishing acknowledges financial support for our publishing activities from the Government of Canada through the Book Publishing Industry Development Program (BPIDP), and the Canada Council.

Contents

Acknowledgements

My thanks to Ralph Getson, Sueann Bailey and Jim Tupper at the Fisheries Museum of the Atlantic; Scott Robson at the Nova Scotia Museum of Natural History; Lynn-Marie Richard at the Maritime Museum of the Atlantic; Gary Shutlak at the Public Archives of Nova Scotia; Wilfred Eisnor of Knickles Studio and Gallery; and Lunenburg resident, Hugh Corkum.

Introduction

This panorama from Hospital Hill is perhaps the earliest photograph taken of Lunenburg. Hospital Hill was named for the Marine Hospital completed there in 1879 which DesBrisay's History of the County of Lunenburg *describes as occupying "a very beautiful site, in full view of the harbor. The building is most suitably arranged, and the sick mariner is well provided for." Some early Lunenburg doctors were Dr. Joseph Steverman who served the community from 1835-1875, Dr. Charles Aitken, d.1895, Drs. Harley, Mack and Gray, and Jeptha Ross. In 1908, Lunenburg had five physicians —R.H. Burrell, E.A. Forbes, H.K. McDonald, Thomas DesBrisay, and Miss Stella Messenger. In addition, the town was served by three dentists, Charles DesBrisay, George A. Polley, and Wilbert Smith.*

In 1995 Lunenburg was designated a World Heritage Site by the United Nations Educational, Scientific, and Cultural Organization (UNESCO), making Lunenburg one of only two World Heritage Towns in Canada. This honour has confirmed modern-day Lunenburg's position as not only a picturesque destination on Nova Scotia's South Shore but also as a town steeped in history that remains richly evident in its architecture, industries, culture, and people. But far from being the tranquil community it is today, Lunenburg's early days were marked by conflict and upheaval.

For more than a century, England and France waged sporadic warfare in the North American colonies. From the early 1600s, Acadia changed hands on several occasions until it was permanently ceded to English rule in 1713 under the Treaty of Utrecht. France at that time retained possession of Isle Royale (Cape Breton), retreating there to fortify the entrance to Quebec, pursue the lucrative cod fishery, and establish a thriving, albeit mostly illicit, coastal trade. Due in large measure to the petitions of Governor William Shirley of Massachusetts in 1747, Halifax was founded two years later to protect against the French stronghold at Louisbourg. Plans were then made to consolidate England's tenuous hold on mainland Nova Scotia by expanding settlement to counter the French Acadian presence.

Wiser for having mistakenly brought, for the most part, a "worthless and lazy, motley lot" from England to settle at Chebucto in 1749, the British turned an imperialist eye to Germany, a country noted for its "frugal, laborious, and industrious people who will not only improve and enrich their property, but pertinaciously defend it." A proclamation was issued and public notices posted in a number of German towns. One hundred and thirty emigrants answered the initial call, enticed with guarantees of generous land grants and settlement allowances in the colonies and a personal desire to escape religious persecution, excessive taxation, and over-population at home. They sailed from Rotterdam to Halifax in 1750, remaining there until 1753 when joined by an additional 1,485 "Foreign Protestants" from areas in Germany, Switzerland, and Montbeliard, a French-speaking territory bordering Switzerland.

The Bay of Fundy region was initially considered for settlement but thoughts of this were discarded because of its large Acadian population and the lack of sufficient troops in Halifax at the time to respond quickly if trouble should arise. Merliguesh on Nova Scotia's south shore had long been the site of Indian encampments, and since the early 1630s a small French colony. Governor Richard Phillips identified it in 1720 as holding promise for future British interests and Edward Cornwallis visited the area in 1749 on his way to Halifax. Isolated from the more numerous French at Fundy and Cape Breton, and situated on an easily defended peninsula with a protected harbour and fertile farming land, the decision was made that here would be the German settlers' new home. Employing a bit of psychology perhaps, Colonel Peregrine Hopson, Governor Cornwallis' newly appointed replacement, chose to call the settlement Lunenburg, in honour of King George II, who held the title Duke of Brunschweig-Luneburg, a German territory from where many of the settlers immigrated.

On June 8, 1753 fourteen transports from Halifax dropped anchor in Merliguesh Harbour. Under the command of Colonel Charles Lawrence and the protection of ninety-two regular British troops and sixty-six Rangers, work began immediately on fortifying defensive positions, clearing land, and erecting temporary shelters. Within ten days, Surveyor General Charles Morris had laid out the town plan, and land grants were distributed by draw using playing cards. Settlers were entitled to a town lot, a garden lot, a three hundred-acre lot and a thirty-acre lot. Each family was to receive seven-hundred feet of boards, five hundred bricks and a proportionate quantity of nails with directives "to enclose his town lot, and erect suitable buildings without delay." Livestock was sent from Halifax a year later—a single cow and one sheep; or six sheep, one pig, and six goats to be allocated for every two families. Single men were given sheep and pigs "according to their respective characters, the most deserving of whom received the largest share."

A militia regiment comprised of all 'able-bodied' males between the ages of sixteen to sixty had been formed before leaving Halifax. Flintlock rifles were issued to the approximately five hundred men and boys fitting the bill and Patrick Sutherland, as Lieutenant Colonel, and Leonard C. Rudolf, as Major, were commissioned to lead them. On June 23 a review of the militia was held at which time sergeants and corporals were chosen. By October 1, 1753 it was reported that 650 men, British soldiers and settler militia, were "well armed."

Thus fortified and provisioned, the fledgling colony settled in. Any French threat was short lived as the Acadians were expelled within two years and Louisbourg fell in 1758 for the second and final time. Skirmishes with the native Mi'kmaq extracted their toll on both sides until peace was signed on November 9, 1761 with Francis Muise, Chief of the Mi'kmaq at LaHave. Then came a sacking of the town and shipping losses to Yankee privateers during the American Revolution and 1812 War. The resilient pioneers persevered through these periods of upheaval, continually working their lands and gradually expanding settlement along the coast and to the interior. By 1795, Lunenburg had only seventy-three homes.

Of the initial 1,453 immigrants, the majority were farmers; records indicate that only two had any previous experience as mariners. While the early seeds of settlement may have been sown in farming, Lunenburg's legacy would soon become deeply rooted in the fishery and sea-borne trade. Only four years after the town's founding, a number of small coasting vessels were supplying Halifax with firewood, and by 1761 Lunenburg was shipping timber, lumber and vegetables to the capital on a regular basis. The fishery was somewhat slower to develop owing to the emphasis on agriculture, but while the golden era of the Grand Banks was still a century away, in 1767 six vessels were providing local needs for fish and fish oil. The years leading into the 1800s were concentrated on the shore fishery. Generally working from small wooden boats within sight of land, two men fished nets for gasperaux, cod, salmon, mackerel, dog fish, eels, haddock, and pollock. Oil made from dog fish livers sold for six to seven dollars a barrel; two men could produce twenty barrels in a season. The rest of the fish was used for fertilizer or pig feed. Other species were dried, pickled, smoked or marketed fresh.

By the early 1800s the shore fishery had become an economic mainstay of Lunenburg but its vessel fishery lagged behind other communities. In 1811, for example, the neighbouring towns of Liverpool, Shelburne, and Barrington sent thirty-nine schooners to deep water but only two sailed from Lunenburg. As demand for fish increased and local merchants realized the economic benefits, the focus shifted. Vessels of varying tonnage were built and outfitted to fish the coasts of Nova Scotia and Labrador. While the initial costs and risks were greater, production out-performed the shore fishery which in the end affected the bottom line, profits. In his *History of the Lunenburg Fishing Industry,* B.A. Balcom writes that by the mid-1820s cod fishing off Labrador "had become the most vital part of the Lunenburg fishery." And in 1829 the town had two brigs, sixteen schooners, and thirteen shallops engaged in vessel fishing for more than three months of the year.

As fishing increased in importance so too did trade. Export markets grew and by 1818 Lunenburg was sending three brigs and four schooners to the British West Indies carrying dried fish, fish oil, and a variety of wood products, lumber, and vegetables. In return, rum, molasses, sugar and coffee were imported, then often re-exported to Halifax, Quebec, and Newfoundland. Coupled with local farm produce, the trade off for fish in Newfoundland was in turn exported from Lunenburg to the West Indies. By 1826, local fish merchants were shipping 280,000 pounds of dried cod annually to the Caribbean aboard nineteen Lunenburg vessels. A number of county communities such as Mahone Bay and LaHave were also actively involved at the time in shipping timber and deal to England. Coastal trade between Lunenburg and Halifax remained strong in cordwood, lumber, and farm produce.

Lunenburg suffered a commercial depression during the 1830s and 1840s brought on, in part, by the collapse of a marine insurance company which had been financed at its start in 1825 by many of the town's affluent merchants and citizens. Another reason for the economic downturn was that Halifax had larger, more established financial firms than Lunenburg and was in a position to back speculative commercial enterprises and extend credit for upwards of six months. Add to this that Lunenburg was not granted 'free-port' designation until 1839—before which all dutiable goods had had to be cleared in Halifax—and times were tough. During the depression years, which spilled over into the early 1850s, direct fish exports from Lunenburg dropped dramatically with trade being re-routed through Halifax. It would appear, however, that county outports and farming communities fared better as they, for the most part, by-passed the town and outfitted vessels or traded produce directly in Halifax. While trade declined during the mid-1800s, Lunenburg's fishery remained strong due in large measure to the fact that many fishermen also farmed, using the combination to see themselves through the lean years.

Lunenburg was well on its way to recovery by the early 1860s thanks to the infusion of working capital from newly established local merchants. James Eisenhauer was one of the primary catalysts, having opened an outfitting business in 1859 for Kingsburg and Tancook fishermen. Soon after this, he sent a schooner to the Labrador fishery and in 1862 had re-established direct trading links with the West Indies. By 1871 James Eisenhauer & Co was considered "the principal business in Lunenburg." Another man responsible for the rise in Lunenburg's fortunes was Lewis Anderson, a business partner of Eisenhauer's, who struck out on his own in 1872 and opened Lewis Anderson & Co. A West Indies merchant for twenty-five years at the time of his death in 1888, he is said to have "occupied a most prominent place amongst the leading townsmen of Lunenburg being known throughout the surrounding country as a man of sterling qualities."

A third firm worthy of mention during this time is Zwicker & Co. which held the distinction of being Canada's oldest fish company still retaining its charter when it closed in 1977. Zwicker & Co opened in 1789, survived the depression, and with W.N. Zwicker as senior partner, moved from its uptown business location in the 1870s to a waterfront wharf where a brisk trade developed in dried fish, lumber, and staves. By 1878, with Eisenhauer, Anderson, and Zwicker leading the way, Lunenburg had eighteen vessels trading in the Caribbean with others sailing to the United States. The value of county exports in fish and fish by-products between 1869-1880 increased nearly four-fold from over $289,000 to $1,176,159.

The fishery was in a constant state of flux in the mid-1800s as it struggled with the vagrancies of the industry—unpredictability of catches, market volatility, foreign competition, governmental incentives and protectionism as well as experimentation with new fishing methods and technology. Despite it all, Lunenburg's shipbuilding industry continued to prosper, turning out bigger and better designed vessels. An earlier reputation of being poorly outfitted and crewed compared to their American counterparts also improved to where it was reported in 1854 that "...those from Lunenburg county in particular were as fine, if not finer, than any of the American vessels." By 1853, there were eighty-five schooners fishing for cod off Labrador, Nova Scotia, and North Bay in the Gulf of St. Lawrence, for mackerel in the coastal waters of Prince Edward Island, Cape Breton, and Bay of Chaleur and for herring off the Magadelen Islands, Labrador coast and bays of Newfoundland. The demand for mackerel was particularly high in the 1850s with fifty-six of the eighty-five vessels

JAMES D. EISENHAUER

A leading Lunenburg citizen, Eisenhauer held a seat in the provincial Legislative Assembly from 1867-1878 and won national election in the county for the Liberal Party in 1887 when he campaigned in favour of free trade with the United States. He lost the seat in 1891 to local Conservative candidate Col. Edwin Kaulbach by 190 votes. McAlpine's 1896 Nova Scotia Directory listed James Eisenhauer as the West India and Commission Merchants; Dealers in Dry and Pickled Fish, Fish Oils, Flour, Meal, Beef, Pork, Salt, and All Fishing Supplies.

ZWICKER & CO. LTD.

E. Fenwick Zwicker, left, and Arthur H. Zwicker pose for a 1910 photo in the company's office. Zwicker & Co. Ltd., was one of the town's most influential fish merchants and West Indies export- ing firms. The family business owned a hardware store on King Street, and waterfront property on Montague Street. Many of the artifacts featured here are on display today at the Fisheries Museum of the Atlantic in Lunenburg.

employed primarily in this branch of the fishery. As the historian Mather DesBrisay commented:

> In the month of October, boats from the Blue Rocks would come into Lunenburg, laden with No. 1 mackerel. They were so abundant that men were engaged along the shore, day and night, in splitting and curing them. The price, when in prime shipping order, was from three to four dollars per barrel; and they could be bought at the stages (taken from the puncheons), split and salted, at the rate of one dollar for each hundred-weight.

The 1870s brought many changes. Destruction of river spawning grounds by nets, spearing, sawmill dams, and refuse destroyed important segments of the shore fishery. The census of 1861, for example, listed Lunenburg County with 168 sawmills and 3,038 nets and seines. By 1877, vessel fishing for mackerel had all but disappeared in the county, owing to low market prices and continual poor catch returns. The cod fishery entered a significant period of transition. Whereas Labrador had been the focal point in the early years, a prolonged downturn in production there switched the emphasis to the fishing banks off Nova Scotia. A change in methodology played a vital role as well.

Handlining from small wooden boats or a vessel's deck had been the norm for decades until the advent of trawl fishing (longlining) during this period. Handlining employed one hook compared to 1,800 on a mile length of trawl. Although Lunenburg fishermen were vocal at the time in their concern for harming the fishery, and also hesitant to endorse new methods, a gradual switch was made as trawls were

the norm in other parts of southwestern Nova Scotia and the United States. A Zwicker Company outfitted schooner, the *Union*, is said to have been the first Lunenburg vessel to break from the tradition of handlining to experiment briefly with fishing trawls in the 1850s at the urging of a Captain Rouchetell from the Jersey Islands. It would be twenty years however before Lunenburg native, Captain Ben Anderson, was credited with introducing trawl fishing to stay. In 1873 five Lunenburg schooners fished trawls on the Western Banks off Sable Island with mixed results. Despite the increased costs in outfitting and bait, as many as forty Lunenburg County vessels were using trawls by 1877 on the Nova Scotia banks and in the Gulf of St. Lawrence, and at the close of the 1870s "only a small minority of Lunenburg vessels continued to sail to Labrador."

As Balcom recounts in his *History of the Lunenburg Fishing Industry*:

CAPT. BEN ANDERSON

Ben Anderson is credited with introducing longlining—better known in Lunenburg as trawl fishing—in 1873 when he sailed in the Dielytris, *along with four other schooners, to the Western Banks off Sable Island. His fellow captains soon became discouraged by the new-fangled devices and left to fish the Labrador coast with the more traditional handlines. Having promised his crew the equivalent of a Labrador trip, Capt. Anderson stuck it out and ultimately landed 1,850 quintals (207,200 pounds) of fish. Considered a successful trip when compared to Labrador numbers (1,200 quintals), Anderson's vessel again fished trawls the following year along with four other schooners, all five returning to port with their holds filled.*

The two decades between 1880 and 1900 can be viewed as an era of consolidation and specialization in Lunenburg's fisheries....A standardized procedure for conducting offshore fishery had been established by the early 1880s. Similarly, a familiar routine existed for financing the fleet, processing the catch and distributing it to markets abroad. The one major change that occurred within the industry toward the end of the nineteenth century concerned the new emphasis placed on the production of dried cod....Other lines of production in the Lunenburg fishery-herring, haddock, halibut, mackerel and canned lobsters-steadily decreased in importance, particularly between 1891 and 1899....Lunenburg's fleet of salt bankers, it would appear, provided the major sources of expansion within the county fishery and they also enabled that fishery to achieve an even greater importance within the local economy.

The key to Lunenburg's growth and prosperity during this era was its self-contained nature. Unlike fisheries in other parts of the province which in the late 1800s experienced a general decline due to the migration of so many workers to other industries, such as mining, railway construction, and manufacturing, such was not the case in Lunenburg. Fishing was 'the' industry. Dozens of town and county shipyards turned out increasing numbers of larger tonnage schooners needed for longer stays during the spring trip to the Nova Scotia banks and the three month voyage to the Newfoundland Grand Banks, which by then was the focus of the summer's fishery. Hundreds of men in county lumber camps and mills produced the ship timbers needed for construction as well as lumber, deal and staves for export to England and the West Indies. Farmers sold produce to outfit the fleet and for local consumption and trade. A variety of marine-related businesses flourished—blockmakers, riggers, sailmakers, shipsmiths, and foundries—as did general labourers, carpenters, and merchants. Unlike their predecessor, both the Lunenburg Marine Insurance Co. Ltd. (1889) and the Fisherman's Marine Insurance Company of Lunenburg (1907) both proved successful, and by the early 1900s were insuring nearly all Lunenburg fishing vessels. Fish makers cured the catches brought to port by salt bankers, then exported aboard square-riggers and schooners, all owned by local interests. A particular source of pride at this time was that the fleet was crewed entirely by men from the Lunenburg area, unlike its U.S. rival from Gloucester which, according to the historian B.A. Balcom, sported "an ancestry of fishermen...made of mongrels. Portuguese, Dutch, Spanish, Italians, etc. help to man the American fleet and there are few nativeborn Americans who find their way to the fishing banks."

Lunenburg sailed into the twentieth century on an economic high but soon faced the winds of change. By then the Spanish West Indies had become Lunenburg's largest market for dried cod. However, the Spanish-American War of 1898 threatened to close trade links when a recently independent Cuba imposed crippling duties on all Canadian imports. This roadblock was circumvented by a practice of selling fish through American consignees who, because of a Cuban-American 1903 commercial treaty, continued trading with Cuba at a lower tariff rate. At the same time, Lunenburg's exports of fish to Puerto Rico, another long-time market, dropped by nearly one-third when the Americans imposed their own protective tariffs in 1901; however, demand in other areas of the Caribbean off-set this loss with higher prices. The muddied political waters settled somewhat between 1912 and 1913 when Canada and the British West Indies reached a long-term trade agreement and the lucrative Puerto Rican market re-opened to dried fish imports with the signing of the Underwood Tariff. Lunenburg's pain was also eased considerably by the decline of its chief fishing competitor. At its height in 1888 the Lunenburg fleet numbered 193 vessels. By comparison, the U.S.-based Gloucester fleet was sending 339 to the fishing banks in the same period. While Lunenburg still outfitted 140 schooners in the early 1900s, Gloucester's bottomed out at approximately 45 in 1906 due in large measure to market losses in the U.S. middle states to the then-developing Pacific Coast fishery.

Despite market uncertainty abroad, Lunenburg's fishery enjoyed record catches from 1900 to 1918. However, they faced growing competition on the home front. The advent of steam was leaving the age of sail in its wake. Halifax was rapidly eroding Lunenburg's export trade with companies like Pickford & Black establishing direct steamship service between the provincial capital and the West Indies. The smaller, slower, wind powered traders could not keep pace. In the 1890s, twenty-five Lunenburg clipper ships of 150–200 tons had plied their trade in the West Indies. During World War One, the only Lunenburg firm sailing south on a regular schedule was Zwicker & Co. By 1922 all shipments of fish out of Lunenburg had ceased. At the same time, Halifax was also cornering the lucrative outfitting market. Whereas a number of Lunenburg businesses had thrived for decades on supplying the necessary stores and supplies for the fleet's spring and summer fishing trips, captains now found it more convenient to outfit in Halifax while unloading their cargoes of fish for export.

Compounding Lunenburg's woes in the early 1900s was the increased importance of fresh fishing. The Canadian market for fresh fish was relatively small: Halifax and Mulgrave on the Canso Strait, supplied Quebec and Ontario from cold storage facilities and rail connectors. On the other hand, the American consumer was demanding fresh fish but this burgeoning market was closed to Canadian interests because of protective U.S. tariffs. It was not long before one-half of the Gloucester fresh fishing fleet was estimated to be crewed by Nova Scotians.

As the historian B.A. Balcom has noted, this was a time of diminishing prospects for the Lunenburg fishery:

> The middle 1900s were a period of stagnation if not decline in the Lunenburg fleet....In 1917 a chronic complaint in the Lunenburg region concerned the emigration of youth who could find no local employment opportunities. Lunenburg fishermen would have been lured across the border by the larger earnings of fishermen there, since fishing was less seasonal. Lunenburg bankers fished slightly over four months of the year while their Gloucester counterparts fished eleven months, and in some cases twelve. Similarly, the average annual salary of a Lunenburg bank fisherman was less than two hundred dollars while those of the Gloucester fisherman was three or four times that amount. As a result of these low earnings and increased opportunities for different employment, the Lunenburg bank fishing fleet experienced a labour shortage in the early 1900s.

Lunenburg's fortunes continued their downward spiral into the 1920s. With the end of the Great War, European and South American economies struggled. Demand for dried fish declined but world production continued unabated, leading to an international glut from large-scale market dumping. Prices plummeted and protectionist tariffs ensued. Iceland and Norway, with their superior-grade dried cod, took over the recovering European market. Canadian and Newfoundland interests shutout overseas, then pressed Lunenburg for what remained in the West Indies. Technology continued to outstrip the sail-driven salt bankers. The first gasoline engines were installed on board Lunenburg schooners in about 1919 for auxiliary power and vessel designs then began changing to minimize the use of sail. Fresh fishing diesel-powered draggers outfitted to scour the ocean bottom with nets soon followed, effectively signalling the death knell of the traditional fishery.

Struggling to forego the inevitable, Lunenburgers instituted a number of changes. Beginning in 1921, the fishing season was lengthened by building cold storage facilities and implementing a "frozen bait trip" in March before the start of the spring trip (so named because bait frozen over the winter was used). During the winter of 1926-27, auxiliary powered schooners began landing weekly catches of fresh fish for processing. Some captains started to fall fish and by 1931, two summer trips instead of one were the norm, thereby allowing catches to be dried and marketed earlier. At the same time, an increased demand for larger fish necessitated the search for newer, more productive fishing grounds off the distant Greenland coast, a practice that continued until the 1940s. Despite all efforts to cling to the salt fishery Lunenburg's bank fishing fleet steadily declined in numbers. Many vessels and men turned to the more lucrative profession of rum-running in the 1920s, so many in fact that "at times, there appeared to be almost as many Lunenburg vessels rum-running as there were fishing." The unpredictability and downturns in the fishery forced increasing numbers of men into other lines of work ashore. Newfoundland crews were recruited to fill the void but to no avail. The Great Depression of the 1930s drove in the last nail and, by 1932, Lunenburg's proud armada of salt bankers, once numbering nearly two hundred, had been reduced to a mere twenty-six vessels.

Like their forefathers before them, Lunenburgers displayed a resiliency born from generations who had faced daily the vagrant mercies of the sea. They were helped by a second world war that jump-started a depression-ravaged economy. Shipbuilding and refitting flourished then as did the fishery. Lunenburg's last remaining shipyard, Smith & Rhuland, was awarded contracts to build rescue boats and tugs. The Lunenburg Foundry went into full production refitting naval vessels and manufacturing related equipment. Fathers, sons, and brothers joined the regular forces, or the merchant navy to maintain the lifelines of the world. Still others sailed into U-boat infested waters to meet the increased demands of the wartime fishery. When Nazi Germany occupied Norway in 1940, Lunenburg opened its doors to six hundred homeless Norwegian sailors from the whaling fleet. The subsequent result was the establishment of Camp Norway, a training centre for the displaced Norwegian navy and army.

Lunenburg experienced a post-war prosperity reminiscent of an earlier era. However, times had changed again. A modern trawler were then able to catch in less than a week what it once took a salt banker three months to land. In 1946 the diesel-powered *Cape North* returned to Lunenburg after a fishing trip of only five-and-a-half days carrying 370,000 pounds of fresh fish, a record for that time. In 1964 National Sea Products built North America's largest fish processing plant. Utilizing the most up-to-date equipment, the new facility had the impressive production capability to process fifty thousand pounds of fish every hour, fillet thirty-five to forty thousands pounds an hour, and a total annual output capacity of eighty million pounds of raw fish. Times were good and through the 1970s and 80s fleets of foreign and domestic factory freezer trawlers pillaged fish stocks to the brink of extinction. From a record catch in 1968 of 1,475,000 tons of cod, annual yields progressively dropped to where only 183,000 tons were taken in 1992. The rape was complete, and a federally imposed moratorium on fishing was instituted that year on northern cod and other ground fish species. The downward spiral continued however into 1996 when fishermen caught only 18,000 tons of cod. The moratorium remains in effect today while politicians and scientists grapple with the collapse of a fishery that put 40,000 out of work, creating social and economic devastation throughout Atlantic Canada where half of the region's 1,300 fishing communities depended entirely on the fisheries.

Lunenburg has fared better than most. Its industrial base and fishery, though scaled back from the heady days of yesteryear, have adapted and diversified to survive. Public awareness of the town's heritage, that began twenty-five years ago with the establishment of a local historical society, culminated in 1995 with Old Town Lunenburg being recognized with World Heritage Site designation. The commercial district, once home to a thriving mercantile system, flourishes again in tourist season.

The waterfront, focal point a century and more ago for fish lots and shipyards set amid a forest of masts, has been minted on the Canadian one hundred dollar bill and is now the site for the Fisheries Museum of the Atlantic, visited in 1998 by more than ninety thousand people.

Historic Lunenburg is the latest in Nimbus Publishing's series of books focussing on the preservation and celebration of Atlantic Canada's town and county heritage. The photographic content of this book centres on the golden age of the fishery under sail, from its rise to prominence in the 1880s, to its demise in the 1930s. As the historian Mather DesBrisay wrote in 1895:

> There is no body of men in this county who deserve to be held in higher regard than the fisherman. The farmers are a hard-working class, and contribute very largely to the general prosperity. They have, indeed, their days of toil, but they have also their nights of sweet repose. The fishermen must work by day and watch by night; and they have to labor in the midst of difficulties and dangers of which landsmen know only by hearsay.

Lunenburg has come to symbolize a way of life now long past. The story of its fishery, shipbuilding, and trade is reflective of Nova Scotia's four hundred coastal towns and hamlets where lives and histories have been shaped by the sea.

Chapter 1

On the Waterfront

WORLD HERITAGE SITE

Salt bankers anchor in the shelter of Lunenburg's Front Harbour while cod cures at the foreground of this ca.1900 panorama. Founded in 1753 by "Foreign Protestants" brought to Nova Scotia by the British, the predominately German settlers soon adapted from a traditional life of farming to one of ship building, fishing and coastal trade. Considered today as "the best preserved North American example of an eighteenth-century British colonial town plan," Old Town Lunenburg, depicted here, retains many of its distinctive features from this early twentieth-century printing.

LUNENBURG HARBOUR CA. 1898

"Why you go to Lunenburg an' get up on one end o' the wharves there an' look down o'er, well it was the same as woods. Spars looked like a forest," recalls a veteran fisherman in Peter Barss' *Images of Lunenburg County*. "The harbours layed full o' vessels—three masters an' four masters—fishin' vessels. An' today there's none.... Yes it was a pretty sight ... 'course was a lot o' men that went out o' these harbours an' never come back too. Their bones are layin' down there yet."

PROCESSING FISH

TOP RIGHT

A busy day on the waterfront is depicted in these two turn-of-the-century photos as dressing crews prepare fish for packing into barrels. A barrel typically held two hundred pounds of herring or mackerel. Note the large box of salt on the back of a wheelbarrow. Salt was vital to the fishery for preserving catches, Lunenburg importing three to four hundred tons annually from Turks Island in the Caribbean. Lunenburg County was known for heavily salting its fish. When Halifax became the focal point for fish exports in the early 1900s, merchants there tried unsuccessfully to convince Lunenburgers to switch to Cadiz salt from Spain because it left less deposits which produced a more widely marketable product. Turks Island salt continued to be used until the mid-1900s when the switch was made to mined salt from Pugwash, Nova Scotia.

BOTTOM RIGHT

In his 1895 history of Lunenburg County Mather DesBrisay provides an informative side-bar in regards to the use of salt. "Salted fish form so large an item of trade in this county that the following will be of interest here: William Buckels was a New Zealand fisherman, and in 1386, he discovered that salt would "keep" fish to that degree that they could be packed for export. In that year he salted herrings and packed them in barrels. The discovery was a great thing for the world, and, at that date, for Dutch commerce. Charles V erected a statue to his memory. Queen Mary of Hungary, while living in Holland, sought out his tomb, and seated upon it, ate a salted herring—and the people of Bierwick celebrated the five hundredth anniversary of the event."

PROCESSING FISH ON THE WATERFRONT (BOTH PHOTOS)

The historic role of cod in the settlement of the Atlantic provinces is comparable to the impact of the fur trade on the rest of Canada. The fishery can be traced back more than five hundred years to the days of John Cabot when the waters were, "swarming with fish, which could be taken not only with the net but in baskets let down with a stone, so that it sinks in the water."

Cod are ground fish once found in bountiful numbers on shallow portions of the Continental shelf known as fishing banks. Of the dozens of banks on our coasts, Lunenburg captains generally favoured Sable Island Bank, Western Bank, Banquero Bank, and LaHave Bank off Nova Scotia and the richest of them all, the Newfoundland Grand Banks. The fishery was at its height in 1888 when Lunenburg County boasted 193 salt bankers and 4,842 fishermen. The value of the Canadian fisheries for that year was over $17,418,510; Nova Scotia's share amounted to more than $7,817,030, Lunenburg County contributing nearly twenty-five percent of this. In 1894, catch totals for Lunenburg were 9,464,000 pounds of codfish alone.

The Lunenburg fleet still numbered 140 vessels in the early 1900s when fish continued to be so plentiful that "they were nailin' cod to the masts." From 1900 to 1920, production estimates put the total catch of the Atlantic fisheries at one billion pounds of cod annually.

FISH LOTS A maze of schooner masts serve as a backdrop to cod flakes along the waterfront. Flakes were long wooden platforms covered with brush on which fish were laid to dry in the sun. They were common throughout Nova Scotia until the 1950s.

As early as 1787, Lunenburg merchants had petitioned for designated 'Fish Lots' on the harbour shore to be used by licensed persons solely for curing fish. Fish Lots were only available to those employing a bank or shore fishing vessel of "not less than thirty tons burthern." In the event that the occupants of such lots did not comply with these provisions, they were given back to the government to be re-licensed. It was hoped these measures would keep the front harbour preserved for activities relating to the fishery.

The small-peaked building in this photo is a fish stores shack where all necessary fishing paraphernalia was kept. When built over the water, as was often the case, the floor boards were left loose so in times of high tides or storms they would lift to lessen the chances of the building being damaged or destroyed.

Lunenburg, N. S., Marine Slip.

An early 1900s postcard depicts two schooners pulled up on the marine slips for repairs The small white piles in the foreground are cod that have been covered over to protect against rain. The following advertisement ran in *McAlpine's Directory for the County of Lunenburg* in 1908:

> We desire to call the attention of all masters and owners of vessels to the fact that we have two railways containing two cradles each, accommodating four vessels at a time of any size up to 500 tons displacement, and drawing 15 feet of water. We guarantee prompt hauling and shall give all outside vessels the preference. We also guarantee to furnish skilled labour and good material at lower rates than any other port in the province. Special rates will be made on application for vessels using the cradles for an extended time. Arthur H. Zwicker, Manager.

The average size of a fishing schooner in the 1850s was approximately fifty tons. As the importance of the banks fishery grew in the 1880s, larger vessels were needed with greater carrying capacity and the capability to remain at sea for months at a time. In 1882 the Canadian government introduced the 'federal fish bounty,' a ship building incentive program that paid between one and two dollars per ton (maximum eighty tons) for any vessel that pursued the fishery for a minimum of three months out of the year. The monies for this came from interest earned on the Halifax Award, a compensation payment under the Treaty of Washington made by the United States to Canada for access to our inshore fishery. The program was a success, the average numbers and size in Lunenburg County increasing from 121 sixty-seven-ton vessels in 1887 to 166 seventy-three-and-a-half-ton vessels in 1899. Statistics show that bounties nearly doubled in the first twelve years for Lunenburg County, beginning with over $18,273 in 1882 and increasing to more than $35,584 by 1893. Overall, there were more than six hundred schooners in the late 1800s sailing out of Nova Scotia ports. By the early 1900s, even larger tonnage vessels were being built, giving rise to the "fisherman"-type schooner which averaged ninety-five to one hundred tons. Featured in this photo is the schooner *Leah Beryl*, built in 1929 at the Smith and Rhuland yards in Lunenburg.

THE SCHOONER *LEAH BERYL*

Crew sizes also increased proportionally under the federal fish bounty program. The bounty was between $3.00 and $7.40 for every fisherman who worked on a fishing vessel for a minimum of three months. At first, this bounty was divided between the owners and crew, but after 1896, it was paid directly to the fisherman. In 1888 each vessel carried between fourteen and sixteen men, depending on the vessel's size. By the end of the century, almost all vessels had a standard crew of twenty-one. A typical crew was comprised of the skipper, cook, salter, header, throater, flunkey or "catchy" (a young boy of ten or so who did odd jobs), and fourteen fishermen divided into seven double dory crews. In 1896 large crews became more popular when the bounty system was changed to reduce the tonnage payment and increase that given to the fishermen.

VESSEL OWNERSHIP

Lunenburg schooner *J.B. Young* and her crew at dockside. She was no doubt named for John Bruno Young (1857-1919) who owned a shipyard from 1905-1919 where the parking lot for the Fisheries Museum of the Atlantic is today.

Prior to 1882, a vessel was generally owned by one of the fish companies or a small investment group of possibly three individuals with one being the majority share-holder. After 1882, with the introduction of the federal fish bounties to encourage the building of larger, and subsequently more expensive vessels, ownership was then divided into sixty-four shares and sold to a number of small local investors to secure the necessary capital. Under this new system, many fishermen often sailed on vessels in which they owned working shares. A managing owner was selected from amongst the investors to oversee the ship's business and protect profits. Some investors came to hold shares in a number of vessels thereby minimizing potential losses. Adams & Knickle for example, outfitters and fish merchants dating to 1887, held ownership in fifteen to twenty vessels.

IRON MEN & WOODEN SHIPS

Schooners were developed in New England in the early 1700s. They were two-masted, their sails rigged fore-and-aft along the length of the vessel. By comparison, a square rigger had its sails covering the width of the ship. In this ca. 1910 photo taken on board the schooner *Frank Adams*, we get a glimpse at some of the iron men who skippered the wooden ships. Those identified are: Capt. 'Long' Albert Himmelman, seated with arms folded; Capt. John Strum, standing to left of Himmelman with hands on hips; Capt. "Jack" (John) Schwartz, standing behind Strum, wearing floppy hat; Capt. Richard Silver, seated to right, holding hat and pipe. Fishing was historically a family tradition as evidenced by a Capt. Freeman Geldert who in 1886 at the age of only twenty-two years old was the youngest of five brothers, all masters of fishing vessels.

As Feenie Ziner attests in her book *Bluenose*, the traits of a successful skipper included impressive mental dexterity:

> A thousand considerations were always joggling about in a skipper's head: his estimate of the weather, the size of the catch in his hold, the number of days he had been out, the price he was likely to fetch at the dock, the condition of his vessel and his men. He read the set of the tides, the lay of the wind, the character of clouds and the behavior of birds as if they were a chart, assigning to each observation the weight of his years of experience. The number of times he made the right decision to go or stay, to try another berth or run home with what he had, to gamble on danger for the sake of a good fare—all these judgments rested entirely with the captain.

A Tranquil Moment

There would no doubt have been moments such as the one depicted in this turn-of-the-century postcard when women paused in silent prayer for the safety of their men folk. DesBrisay remarks that "During their absence at their work, long intervals must pass when their families cannot hear from them. The howling wind and the roar of the ocean frequently sadden the inmates of their sea-girt homes, by reminding them that those they love may be lost amidst the contending elements." Many fishermen spent the better part of the year at sea. By the 1880s the Lunenburg fishing fleet was making two voyages a season, a spring trip to the banks off Nova Scotia from March to the end of May, then a longer summer trip to the Newfoundland Grand Banks from the first of June to the last of September. With the end of fishing, crews were then needed for fall and winter freighting trips aboard schooners and square riggers carrying fish, lumber, staves, and produce to the Caribbean. One Lunenburg captain, Edward Gerhardt, made more than 230 voyages in the West India trade between 1869-1895.

Lunenburg Wharves

Dried cod awaits shipment on the Lunenburg waterfront, ca 1918. Trade was vital to the Lunenburg economy from the days of its founding. During the early to mid-1800s, exporters sold fish to the Halifax market for $1.50 to $2.50 per quintal (112 pounds). In 1818, forty-eight coasting vessels made as many as three trips each to Halifax within the span of one month. Statistics show that by 1826 a lucrative export business had developed. Cod fish was then, and continued to be, the county's dominant export commodity amounting to more than two million pounds for that year. In 1861 it had increased to seven million, and by 1882 to more than eleven million pounds. A significant quantity of wood products were also exported during the 1800s including boards, staves, shingles, planks, timber, deal, spars and lathwood. The bulk of farm produce shipped was comprised of potatoes, cheese, and cabbage.

A late 1800s photo depicts men standing in the rigging, booms and yards of the three-masted topsail schooner *Morales* and brigantine *Clio* at the Eisenhauer & Co. wharves. Rum, sugar, molasses and coffee were historically the four commodities most often brought back from trading trips in the Caribbean. In 1826, Lunenburg's two largest imports amounted to 37,956 gallons of rum and 33,018 gallons of molasses. Additional imports for that year included among many things 190 straw hats and bonnets, cordage, paint, coal tar, spikes and nails, iron bars and bundles, canvas, cotton wool, hides, putty, glass, twine, Lignum-vitae, fishing tackle, lime juice, oranges, and lemons.

LUNENBURG VESSELS MADE THEIR MARK

A square-rigged vessel tied up to Zwicker's Wharf with company stores in the background, ca. 1900. During the 1880s there were seventeen square-riggers trading out of Lunenburg. Considered small (an average size being 150 tons) when compared to the great sailing ships from Yarmouth and Halifax, they nevertheless made their mark. One Lunenburg square-rigger, the *Geneva*, built by James Maxner, established a sailing record for that time, completing a 14,000 mile trip from Halifax around the Cape Horn to Vancouver in 110 days.

THE ZWICKER-OWNED *Sceptre*

TOP RIGHT

The Zwicker-owned *Sceptre* shown here ice-bound in Front Harbour, was renowned for completing a round-trip in 1888 from Lunenburg to Puerto Rico and Turk's Island in thirty-two days. The durable vessel also completed eight return trading voyages to the West Indies within fourteen months. In all, the *Sceptre* made 121 voyages to the West Indies, fifty-seven of them under the command of Capt. Henry Burke. The *Sceptre* sank in 1913 after a collision.

LLOYD GEORGE, ONE OF NOVA SCOTIA'S MOST FAMOUS SCHOONERS

BOTTOM RIGHT

The schooner *Lloyd George* lies on her side in Lunenburg Harbour after falling off the marine railway slip, 1919. This was seen as a bad omen by some which was proven out a year later when she was lost December 14, 1920 while carrying 179,200 pounds of fish to the Virgin Islands. Built in 1910 at the McGill shipyards in Shelburne for Zwicker & Co. the speed of the *Lloyd George* was legendary. The *Halifax Herald* carried the following entry on December 21, 1920: "This vessel was one of the best known and most famous of all Nova Scotia schooners. She had many exceptionally fast passages to her credit. On one, in particular, she did the round trip from Lunenburg to Ponce in twenty-six days, discharging at Ponce, proceeding to Turks Island and taking on salt. She made the run home from Turks Island in seven days. It is doubtful if this record has ever been equalled or bettered by a schooner."

THE ZWICKER-OWNED *SCEPTRE*

LLOYD GEORGE, ONE OF NOVA SCOTIA'S MOST FAMOUS SCHOONERS

WORKING THE DOCKS

Unloading dried fish from wagons to be stored in waterfront warehouses until shipment. Eight wharves appear on an 1879 Bird's Eye View Map of Lunenburg, each labelled with its owner's surname reflecting some of the town's prominent mercantile families of that time—Eisenhauer, Anderson, Zwicker, Rudolf, Jost, Lindsay, Finch, and Morash. Some Lunenburg residents listed their profession in early business directories as wharfinger, a person who kept a wharf for landing goods and collected wharfage fees.

Two men carry dried cod up a ramp on wooden litters called handbarrows ca. 1900. Gangs of labourers were needed to meet the back-breaking demands of loading and unloading the hundreds of vessels that docked annually in Lunenburg. The

work generally fell to the ship's crew for which they did not receive any additional pay. Other times it was done by young boys, or men past the age of going to sea. With a handbarrow capable of holding 224 pounds, a tump line over the shoulders to the handles was then often used to lighten the load. For this, workers in the late 1920s were remunerated at the rate of thirty to thirty-five cents an hour—a good wage considering men working the woods were paid one dollar a day.

NOVA SCOTIA CENTRAL RAILWAY

Train cars of lumber await unloading on the Government Wharf in Lunenburg, ca. 1916. Work began in the 1870s on the Nictaux and Atlantic Railway in Annapolis and Lunenburg Counties. After many years of delays, the line was finally completed in 1899 connecting Middleton with Bridgewater and Lunenburg. Stations were located throughout the county at Lunenburg, Mahone Bay, Block-House, Bridgewater, Northfield, Riversdale, New Germany, and Cherryfield. Then known as the Nova Scotia Central Railway, it was bought out in 1903 by the Halifax and South Western Railway. Coupled with a steamship service, which by the late 1890s connected Lunenburg with Yarmouth and Halifax on a regular schedule, the railway opened up Lunenburg to the then-developing tourism industry, its trademark a century later.

EARLY TUGBOATS

Maggie

The steam tug *Maggie* was built by William F. Whitney of Lunenburg in November 1891 for Capt. George Naas who is credited with starting the first towing business in Lunenburg Harbour. The *Maggie*, named after Naas's daughter, was one of several family-owned tugs. However, she lacked the power needed to move big sailing vessels to and from their anchorages and was subsequently used primarily as a water lighter. Capt. Naas sold the vessel in 1904 and two years later she was totally destroyed by fire at Canso. Naas was also responsible for building the first marine slip in Lunenburg to haul out his steamers for refitting.

Mascotte

Built in 1896 at Dartmouth, N.S. for the Acadia Sugar Refinery, the *Mascotte* was used in 1902 as a summer ferry between Mahone Bay and Chester, typically carrying as many as one hundred passengers. It was purchased later that year by Capt. George Naas who then ran it as a harbour tug and a ferry between Lunenburg and Bay Port, Corkum's Island and Cross Island until 1934.

END OF AN ERA

By the start of the 1919 fishing season, Lunenburg had three trawlers built at LaHave and Shelburne to meet consumer demand for fresh fish which had been steadily growing since the early 1900s. Although owned and operated by Lunenburg interests the new vessels generally sailed out of other ports. The *Promotion*, featured here landing her catch of fresh fish at LaHave, worked for a company in nearby Liverpool, Queens County. Her time was short lived however, being run down by the French liner *La Lorraine* on September 1, 1919, without loss of life.

First powered by steam—then diesel—trawlers or draggers as they were also known, scoured the ocean bottom with bag-like nets to catch cod and other ground species for the fresh fish market. At first the net was fished from the vessel's side but later towed astern. Lunenburg was hesitant to adopt the use of trawlers, its dorymen upset with the prospect of abandoning their traditional handlines and trawls for a method they feared would harm the fishery. However, times were changing and with Halifax, Lockeport, Canso, Mulgrave, and Port Hawkesbury moving to trawlers and upwards of one hundred similar vessels from Europe and the United States fishing off the East Coast, Lunenburgers had no choice but to adapt. The number of fishing schooners steadily decreased from this point onward, dropping below one hundred in 1925 for the first time in decades, "a measure the fleet never regained." With the Great Depression came a dramatic decline, only twenty-six remaining by 1932 from a fleet that once numbered nearly two hundred. For all intents and purposes, the classic salt banker had by this time sailed into history.

Landing halibut at Lunenburg Sea Products Ltd. from the schooner *Jean & Shirley*. The end was near for the traditional salt fishery at the time of this photo. Foreign competition, steam trawlers, new technology, and increased market demand for fresh and frozen fish would forever change the face of the Atlantic fishery. A sign of the times was the establishment of Lunenburg Sea Products Ltd. in 1926, a subsidiary of W.C. Smith & Co. Ltd., which introduced cold storage and rail facilities, a cannery and fish meal plant and the innovative process of filleting, to compete in the fresh and frozen fish market. An artificial dryer was also installed to improve the finishing of partially sun-dried fish. In the mid-1940s, Lunenburg Sea Products was merged into National Sea Products which, over the next three decades, would employ 3,500 workers, own more than forty trawlers, build North America's largest processing plant, and market its High Liner trademark fish products into a household name.

MARJORIE & DOROTHY   From the time gasoline engines were first installed on-board Lunenburg schooners ca. 1919 dependence upon sail increasingly diminished as future designs incorporated auxiliary power. The *Marjorie & Dorothy*, featured here on the marine slip, was typical of the "Lunenburg-type" schooner of the 1930s. Built in 1934, she featured a rounded bow of an earlier "knockabout" design, a wheelhouse aft and carried only enough sail "to be 'hove-to' when at sea, or to keep her moving without using the engine." She was outfitted with a 300-horsepower diesel motor, capable of ten knots, the largest of any Lunenburg vessel up to that time.

LAST OF THE SALT BANKERS

Building the *Theresa E. Connor* and *Lilla B. Boutilier* at the Smith & Rhuland yards, ca. 1938. Both a salt and fresh fishing vessel during her career, the auxiliary-powered *Theresa E. Connor* was the last of the salt bankers, surprisingly making her final dory fishing trip in 1962, after which time it was no longer possible to find a crew to man her boats. She was purchased in 1966 by the Town of Lunenburg and turned into a floating museum in 1967 as a Centennial of Confederation project. The vessel today forms an integral part of the Fisheries Museum of the Atlantic on the Lunenburg waterfront.

Chapter 2

Streetscapes

A BRITISH COLONIAL TOWN

Lunenburg was designed on the "model plan" of British colonial towns involving three main components—a parade, space for public buildings, and expansive common land. In 1753, surveyor General, Charles Morris, divided the settlement into six divisions named after the officers in charge: Zouberbuhler, Creighton, Morreau, Rudolf, Straesburgher, and Steinfort. Each division consisted of eight blocks, a block comprising fourteen lots, each lot measuring only forty-feet wide by sixty-feet long. Streets were laid out to run parallel and perpendicular to the harbour. At the town's center was a four block Grand Parade, bisected by King Street, shown here looking southwest toward Front Harbour. Eighty feet in width, King stands in sharp contrast to Lunenburg's narrow streets. Contained within the parade are a number of historic areas and buildings including the town's first church and the site of an early Academy.

PRINCIPAL STREETS OF OLD TOWN LUNENBURG

Mather DesBrisay's 1895 *History of the County of Lunenburg* lists the town's principal streets at its founding as being Cornwallis, Duke, King, Prince, Hopson, Lawrence, York, Fox, Townsend, Cumberland, Lincoln, Pelham, and Montague. Many of the streets, like Pelham featured here ca. 1905, were a mix of residential and business. Pelham, for example, featured establishments ranging from J.H. Wilson's Boots & Shoes, Bailly Bros. Bread and Fancy Cake Bakers, Mrs. Tamer Hirtle's Boarding House, Stephen Myra's Butcher Shop, and C.W. Lane, Barrister, to Solomon Knickle's and Timothy Young's Livery & Feed Stables, Frank Young's Trucking, and Thomas Hamm, Sailmaker. Early photos indicate the double sleigh was probably used by one of several truckmen or teamsters in Lunenburg to transport logs for milling or blocks of ice to winter storage.

KING STREET, CA. 1900

TOP RIGHT

Looking up the west side of King Street from corner of Montague Street toward northwest corner of Pelham Street. The close proximity of these homes to each other is indicative of the tight grid pattern laid out for early defensive purposes in the Old Town section of Lunenburg. The large house to the far right was built in 1825 for a sea captain. It was sold in 1851 to one of Lunenburg's most influential merchants W.N. Zwicker, and the home remained in the Zwicker family for well over one hundred years.

KING STREET (BOTH PHOTOS)

A continuing view up King Street toward the Town Hall and Court House with the spire of St. Andrew's Presbyterian Church showing to the left. Visible at the top of the hill is the steeple of St. Norbert's Roman Catholic Church. When Lunenburg was settled in 1753 there were not enough Catholic settlers to warrant building a church and it was nearly a century before St. Norbert's was erected around 1840. The church was closed from 1890-1935 when congregational numbers again dropped to where the building could not be maintained. In the foreground of this photo, two ladies stand in front of the entrance to an establishment on the corner of Lincoln Street displaying prominent window banners advertising "Ice Cream" and "Try Our California Tangerette, Non-Alcoholic-Five Cents." This building, which may have been Mark Rhuland's ice cream parlour, was torn down in 1950.

VIEW FROM GALLOWS HILL

The prosperous, picturesque view featured in this early 1900s postcard was a far cry from the days of Lunenburg's founding. Then, defense was a priority and homes were little more than shanties. Twelve block-houses were built at strategic sites in the town and the surrounding countryside with a picket palisade crossing the peninsula from Front to Back Harbours. Garrison block-house on Gallows Hill would have given a commanding view of the harbour as can be seen from this photo. Fort Boscawen, which once stood on Battery Point in the distance to the left, protected the harbour approaches.

According to historian Mather DesBrisay, 319 houses and ten huts comprised the original settlement, most being temporary dwellings, "constructed of round poles and were about six feet square in the post, and eighteen or twenty feet square outside. Others were of hewed timber, about six inches through. The roofs of many were thatched. The doors and shutters were made of two-inch plank, when it could be had, and fastened with iron bolts."

LUNENBURG'S OLDEST HOME
More than four hundred buildings comprise Lunenburg's historic Old Town section. At present, only eight have been identified dating to the 1700s. The Romkey House, pictured here, is reputed to be the oldest existing house in Lunenburg, thought to have been built sometime around 1779 but the exact construction date and builder are not known with certainty. Records confirm its existence dating to at least 1783 when it was owned by the James A. Anderson family, United Empire Loyalists from Shelburne. It was later purchased by Edward Dowling in 1860 and served for many years as Lunenburg's Customs Office.

The first permanent homes built in Lunenburg were generally one-and-a-half-storey colonial Cape Cod designs. Their construction reflected Lunenburg's Germanic and Swiss roots using a European technique known as "coulisse" to build the walls—three-inch planks were placed one on top of the other and slotted into grooved corner posts. The exterior was then covered over with shingles or clap boards and the interior with finishing boards. Coulisse—while still found in Germany and Switzerland—is believed to be unique to Lunenburg in North America.

Lunenburg is an architectural mosaic reflecting in its homes the rise to prominence and affluence the town achieved during the prosperous days of fishing and trade in the late nineteenth century. Many styles are represented, evolving from the simple Cape Cod to large two-storey Georgians in the early 1800s, to French Second Empire, Victorian Gothic and Italianate during the 1870s–1880s.

French Second Empire-style home, built ca. 1883-90 for fishermen George and Samuel Tanner.

Italianate design built ca. 1876 for boot & shoe merchant, developer Henry Wilson.

The 'Lunenburg Bump' is a distinctive Lunenburg characteristic derived "from the five-sided Scottish dormer, which in the hands of Lunenburg builders was extended out and down from the roof to create an overhang or frontpiece above the central doorway." Blacksmith Edwin Bailly had this home built in the 1880s with a modified Italianate Bump design.

A residential section of Lunenburg known as Newtown, looking west along Cumberland Street to the intersection of Falkland and Dufferin Streets where the railroad crossed. Beyond the town's original lots laid out in 1753 there were areas set aside in the British tradition for common lands and lots for gardening and farming. As the original Old Town, Lunenburg prospered and the population grew in the era of the Banks fishery and West Indies trade, expansion took place on these common lands to the east and west. Subsequently named Newtown during the building boom of the mid-to-late-nineteenth century, the area to the northwest of Front Harbour was developed into an eighty lot subdivision in 1862 which was enlarged in 1878.

A HUB OF ACTIVITY

A busy day along Water Street (Montague St.) is shown in this ca. 1900 photo. Water Street, running parallel to the harbourfront wharves and slip ways, was the hub of Lunenburg's fishing, mercantile, and shipbuilding industries. An array of craftsmen, businesses, and merchants plied their trade including block makers, riggers, shipwrights, blacksmiths, sail makers, hardware manufacturers, and suppliers, a coal company, coopers, ship chandlers, and exporting firms involved in the fish and lumber trade.

LUNENBURG'S COMMERCIAL DISTRICT

Lincoln Street, featured in this turn-of-the-century postcard, was Lunenburg's primary commercial district. Mrs. Martin Born is said to have been the settlement's first shop keeper which she operated from the family loghouse near the Presbyterian church. In a heavy birch trunk she kept "a depository for calicoes, ribbons, needles and other goods supplied by Mrs. Born's sisters residing at Halifax." From these humble beginnings, Lunenburg grew by 1827 to include twenty-two stores selling general stocks of British and West Indies goods imported from Bermuda, Demerara, Berbice,

St. Lucia, Grenada, Antigua, St. Kitts, Jamaica, Montserrat, St. Martins, Liverpool, England, New Brunswick, and Newfoundland.

LINCOLN STREET, CA. 1900

A partial list of the businesses on Lincoln for 1908 as registered in McAlpine's Directory for the County of Lunenburg included: R.A. Backman, Harness Store & Livery Stable; Wm A Banks, Eye Specialist; J & G. Berringer Butchers, Provisions and Groceries; Freeman Boliver, Cabinet Maker & Picture Framer; Harold Burns, Confectionary & Fruit; A.W. Ernst, Hairdresser; Mrs. Isaac Gate's Boarding House; B.G. Herman Grocery; Charles Himmelman, Watchmaker & Jeweller; J.A. Hirtle & Co., Merchant Tailors & Gents Furnishings; L.A. Hirtle, Photographer, Pianos, Organs, etc.; James S. Holland, Watchmaker, Jeweller & Fancy Goods; Wah Hop Chinese Laundry; Wm. Knickle, Barber; Lunenburg Glass Co. Ltd.; Lunenburg Marine Insurance; S.E. Mack Paints, Brushes, Oils, Varnishes, Wall Paper; Mayflower Steam Laundry; J.J. McLachlan & Son Dry Goods, Boots & Shoes; MacLean & Matheson, Barristers; J.S. Meisner, Household Furniture, Upholstery Work; George Miller Restaurant; Minto Pharmacy; E.L. Nash, Druggist, Books, Stationery & Fancy Goods; C.A. Oxner, Hairdressing, Bath & Billard Rooms; F. Rafuse Restaurant; J.J. Rudolf & Co. Hardware; J. Joseph Rudolf, Dry Goods; G.W. Silver, Dry Goods, Gents & House Furnishings, Millinery; J.W. Smeltzer, Butcher & Grocer; Freeman Smith, Boots, Shoes, Slippers & Rubbers; B. Wright, Grocer; A.J. Wolf, Commission Merchant, Ship & Insurance Broker; W.A. Zwicker, Clothing, Hats & Caps.

CAPT. GEORGE NAAS WITH HIS HORSE- DRAWN SLEIGH

Capt. George Naas poses with his horse-drawn sleigh on Lincoln St., ca. 1900. Sleighs were built locally by J. Rafuse who opened his Lunenburg carriage and sleigh factory in the 1880s. There were few horses in the early 1800s. To attend 'divine service' on Sunday's, people walked from Bridgewater to Lunenburg (twelve miles). John Thompson, an elderly Bridgewater resident recalled in 1888, "I had to walk there to post letters for England, and when I expected any, had to go there for them." When horses later became more numerous, ladies "frequently rode many miles on a pillion behind their husbands."

LUNENBURG COUNTY'S FIRST 'GIG'

Lunenburg County's first 'gig'—a light, two-wheeled vehicle with wooden springs "so placed as to make them comparatively easy"—made its appearance in the mid-1800s. Its owner is recorded as having been Rev. Thomas Shreve, the Anglican minister in Mahone Bay.

LEWIS A. HIRTLE AND HIS FOUR-WHEELED CARRIAGE

Lunenburg photographer Lewis A. Hirtle poses in his carriage outside Lunenburg's Town Hall ca. 1900. Dr. John Bolman, a British army surgeon who came to Lunenburg after the American Revolution, is credited with importing the first four-wheeled carriage around the same time as Rev. Shreve's gig. In 1862 there were sixty-two carriages built in the county. In DesBrisay's 1895 Lunenburg County History an elderly resident remembered when "the roads made at first were rough and very narrow. We had often to cut notches in the large stumps when wagons were first used, to let the hubs pass through."

PASSENGERS IN A FORD MODEL-T, CA. 1915 Automobiles first came to Lunenburg around 1908. This Ford Model T, ca.1915, is said to have been owned by a Rev. Halsam, seated in the front passenger's side. In 1901 an Act was passed providing for street paving on a cost shared basis between residents and the town. Exactly when Lunenburg first had paved roads is unclear but for the most part paving in Nova Scotia did not begin until the 1920s.

KINGS HOTEL

Lunenburg offered several boarding houses and hotels for the weary traveller. The Kings Hotel, at the corner of Pelham and Duke Streets, was perhaps the town's finest, built in 1866 by Henry King who catered principally to the travelling salesman of that era. From its beginnings the hotel was the stopping point for the stage coach and in later years provided pick-up and drop-off service at the railway terminus.

Sporting twenty-eight bedrooms along with separate drawing and writing rooms, a dining room and one private and two public parlours, the Kings Hotel was the social centre of Lunenburg for dances and concerts. In 1928 the hotel came under new management, the Lunenburg Hotel Company, and the name was changed to *Ich Dien*, meaning I Serve. The new venture lasted only ten years however and by World War Two the building was no more than an "empty shell." During the war, it was taken over by the Greek government for a Seaman's Manning Pool and then served briefly as a navigation school for those studying for their Captain's tickets. By the mid-1950s, with the glory years well behind it and in a run-down condition, the hotel was demolished, leaving only a vacant lot which then was used for parking.

Group shot taken in front of *The Progress Enterprise* Newspaper, Montague Street, ca. 1904. Standing on boardwalk, left to right are: Melda Walters, Nellie Miller, Maggie McKinnon, unknown, Dick Gilfoy. Back row: Charlie Miller, Pearl Knickle, Laura Knickle, Mr. Meichszner. Lunenburg had several newspapers: *The Progress Enterprise* (1878-present), was a weekly publication covering "a miscellany of literature, education, temperance, and general information." Originally called the *Lunenburg Progress* and printed by a variety of publishers early on, it was sold to William Duff in 1900 who merged it with his *Bridgewater Enterprise*. Lunenburg Printing & Publishing put out another weekly newspaper, the *Argus*, ca. 1889-1908, which was "devoted to the fishing, agricultural, mining, and commercial interests of Lunenburg county." Two daily tabloids followed, the *Daily News*, ca. 1899-1918 and the *Malagash News*, ca. 1914-1920. They amalgamated in 1918 for approximately two years. There were two other short-lived ventures, the *Semiweekly News*, ca. 1907-1918 and the *Weekly News*, ca. 1909-1918.

It was customary for newspapers to square off at election times. In Lunenburg, *The Progress Enterprise* sided with the federal Liberals while the *Argus* promoted the virtues of the Conservatives. So myopic along party lines were the two that even the printing of obituaries it has been said were selected according to the deceased's political affiliation.

Chapter 3

Business & Industry

SHIP CHANDLERS

W.C. Smith & Co. were one of several Lunenburg ship chandlers involved in the business of provisioning and outfitting vessels. Others of note were Zwicker, Eisenhauer, Anderson, Rudolph, and Adams & Knickle. Vessels were provided supplies, equipment, and bait on credit from an outfitter or chandlery which, in turn, received financing from the bank. When the vessel returned to port, fish-makers were hired to cure the catch. The owner or managing partner of the vessel then negotiated a selling price with a fish merchant. If market demand was low, the fish would be held until such time as when the selling price improved. In many cases, the entire process was controlled by the ship chandlers who not only outfitted vessels they owned controlling shares in but they were also in the business of buying and exporting fish. There were as they say no poor outfitters or captains, only fishermen who often waited months to be paid. In the interm, they lived on credit from the company stores so that when it came time to settle accounts, little money actually changed hands.

SHIPBUILDING CA. 1910

By 1895, thirteen thousand boats consisting of whalers, dories, skiffs, flat, keel and centre-board boats had been constructed in Lunenburg town. The principal boat-builders were James Maxner, William Morash, Stephen Morash, Arthur Oxner, Conrad and Anderson, William Whitney, and Alexander Anderson. A considerable number were built by Mr. Joseph McLachlan.

Other early Lunenburg builders of note were John F. Leary, David Smith, John Smith, John and Hibbert Young, Joseph Young, and Peter Young. Many of these men also built vessels in other parts of the county.

The last of the Lunenburg yards was Smith & Rhuland Ltd. started in 1900 by Richard Smith and George Rhuland. Before it was sold in 1975, the renowned shipyard built more than 270 vessels including the Bluenose and a number of rum runners. Three replicas were launched as well near the end of its tenure: H.M.S *Bounty* (1960), *Bluenose II* (1963) and H.M.S. *Rose* (1970).

CAULKING AND HAWSING

BOTTOM RIGHT

When making a vessel watertight, a worker might be caulking or hawsing. On deck, these five men using irons and mallets, were said to be caulking. Pictured in the caulking gang are, from left to right: Charlie Buckmaster, Willis Oickle, Aubrey Deal (front), unknown, Harold Morash, boss caulker. The strips of water-proofing driven between the planks were comprised of one strand of cotton and two of oakum.

When working below deck, similar work would be done but with much larger tools. This was called hawsing. In this photo, Fred Rhuland, left, (son of shipyard owner George Rhuland) swings a 'hawsing beetle' maul while an unidentified worker holds the hawsing iron.

Visible along the hull are the ends of the round wooden pegs used to nail planking to the ship's frame. In the 1800s, men shaped and sold the long hardwood pegs called treenails costing ten dollars a thousand. The traditional skills of the shipwright continue to be in demand today as evidenced by the arrival in port this past spring of the Norwegian tall ship *Anna Kristina* whose skipper chose Lunenburg because "of the facilities...you can get anything you want here to refit a wooden ship."

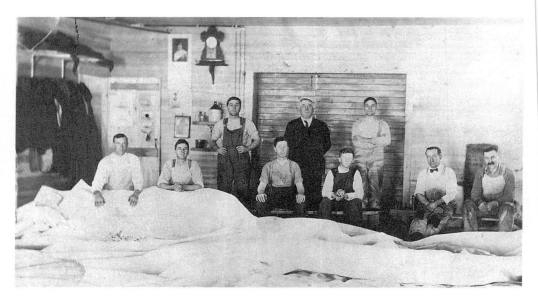

Hewitt and Adams are one of the earliest sailmakers on record in Lunenburg, setting up business in 1865, with annual revenues of $10,000. In 1896 there were eight sailmakers operating in and around Lunenburg-Henry Adams, Thomas Hamm, John Arenburg, William Burns, Charles Hewitt & Co., Roland Naas, Henry Selig, and Arthur Hebb. Under the guidance of a master sailmaker, a pattern was generally laid out on the sail loft floor. From this, numbered panels or cloths of canvas were cut and then sewn together by a group of sailmakers using needles of varying sizes, and a leather hand protector called a sail maker's palm.

Making sails was a highly skilled profession requiring an apprenticeship before qualifying in the trade. By the early 1900s, treadle powered Singer sewing machines were becoming common and made the sailmaker's job considerably less labour-intensive.

A. DAUPHINEE & SON BLOCK SHOP

A.
**DAUPHINEE
& SON
BLOCK SHOP,
MONTAGUE
STREET**

BOTTOM LEFT

Alfred Dauphinee Sr. and his son George stand amid an array of blocks and parts, barrels, bait, and trawl tubs ca. 1910. The business was started in the 1850s by Peter Loye (1829-1903) who went to sea at an early age, then apprenticed with George Acker from Second Peninsula to learn the block-making trade. Several tons of lignum-vitae were imported annually from the American tropics to build the blocks, or pulleys, because its extremely hard qualities were well suited to the heavy use incurred on board vessels and around the docks. In 1884, his son-in-law Alfred B. Dauphinee joined him in the business making blocks, deadeyes, trawl and bait tubs, dory bailers and ice mallets. In 1898 Alfred's son George came into the family firm and Peter Loye retired. The name was then changed to A. Dauphinee & Son and one hundred years later the firm continues in operation at Second Peninsula, turning out an array of items including yacht blocks, oars, and bailers.

THE LUNENBURG DORY

Dories were used off our coasts as early as the sixteenth century by Basque and French fishermen. It was not until the early 1870s, however, with the development of the banks fisheries, that Lunenburg craftsmen began to build dories. Over the years a keen rivalry developed between Lunenburg and neighbouring Shelburne as to which town turned out the best boat. Shelburne became more celebrated perhaps for the sheer number of dories built there but the design characteristics of both places were similar.

The most significant difference was in their method of construction. Lunenburg-built dory frames were made from single pieces of wood which incorporated the natural curve of a tree's root or branch. Shelburne boat-builders, on the other hand, cut construction time by joining two pieces of wood using a galvanized metal dory clip said to have been invented and patented in the late 1870s by Shelburne's Isaac Coffin Crowell. Some feel the single-piece

frames were stronger than those built using metal clips. Two of Lunenburg's earliest dory builders were John Anderson and Edward Conrad who operated their business from around 1870 to 1900. The cost of a dory then was just over sixteen dollars.

WASHING FISH

When Lunenburg schooners returned to port with holds packed with green salted fish, their cargoes were turned over to the 'fish makers' whose job it was to cure the catch for sale. Spring and early fall were the best drying seasons as fish were prone to sunburn in the summer months. The curing process generally took three weeks. The salted fish were washed and scrubbed as pictured here, before being stacked in piles to drain the pickle.

DRYING FISH

The next step was to spread the fish on flakes to dry, turning them regularly to prevent sunburn, or keeping them covered when it rained. Near the end of three weeks, the fish would again be piled to 'sweat out' what moisture remained, then laid out to finish drying. Making fish was a specialized trade. Different markets required varying grades of dryness and the fish-maker had to ensure he knew for what market a particular catch was being dried.

LUNENBURG CURE Lunenburg produced a "soft" cure of fish meaning it retained a higher moisture content than the "hard" cured variety from areas like the Gaspé and Labrador. Lunenburgers preferred the soft cure because it was cheaper to produce and gave a greater quantity of marketable fish. For example, a dry quintal (112 pounds) of fish for export required 165 pounds of green salted Lunenburg fish compared to 224 pounds of Newfoundland fish for a hard cure. Lunenburg cured fish, while inexpensive and well-preserved, was considered low grade by world standards because it lacked an "attractive whiteness" preferred in European and North American markets. This was caused by the practice of not immediately bleeding the catch or white-naping it—removing its black membrane—when cleaning. Heavy salting in the vessel hold to preserve it also tended to occasionally redden the flesh, further devaluing its market price. To lightly or slack salt the catch would not have been practical for the Lunenburg schooners fishing the Grand Banks because this would have required frequent trips home to keep the fish from spoiling. Some captains compensated for this by going ashore in Newfoundland and curing their catch while remaining on the banks to fish. Lunenburg fish merchants were not overly concerned at any rate because their markets were in the Caribbean, principally Puerto Rico, where the lower-grade cure was popular.

**CUTTING &
PACKING
FISH, CA.
1890**

After the curing process was complete, fish were marketed in bulk or packed for sale in wooden boxes or barrels. Black Bros & Co. Ltd. was an outfitting and fish drying business with its main office in Halifax and branch offices in Labrador, and LaHave, Lunenburg County. The LaHave operation, pictured here, was involved primarily in the processing of boneless and shredded fish and by 1905 had fifty employees producing ten thousand pounds of fish daily.

In 1906, Black Bros. amalgamated with the Lunenburg firms of Lewis Anderson & Co. and Hirtle & Rafuse to form Atlantic Fish Companies. Four years later Atlantic Fish Companies became a branch of Robin, Jones & Whitman, another Lunenburg salt fish business. At this time, the production of shredded fish was discontinued. However, market demand necessitated a temporary re-opening of the LaHave plant but with a twenty-five per cent increase in prices. The operation was soon moved to the Robin, Jones & Whitman property on Montague Street at the eastern end of Lunenburg. Fish were then sun-dried on site and packaged for markets in Toronto, Montreal, and Quebec. By 1917, J.F. MacKay of Northfield, Lunenburg County was benefiting from the economic spin-off of the salt-fish business, selling $12,000 a year in wooden packaging boxes to Robin, Jones & Whitman.

E. Bailly's Blacksmiths Shop, Lunenburg, N. S.

BLACK-SMITHING WAS A FLOURISHING TRADE

A century ago, Lunenburg was known as having "smithies at the end of every block on the waterfront." In 1889, one noted blacksmith, Edward Bailly, was said to have on behalf of Messrs. Cantelope, of North-West tended to the same horse for twenty-three years, having used 736 shoes and 5,888 nails.

Employing as many as eight men sometimes as blacksmith apprentices and labourers, Lunenburg shops carried on not only the traditional trade of the smithy but specialized as shipsmiths. As such they forged an array of fittings and ironworks for sailing vessels including anchors and chains, fastenings and bands for the rudder, masts, and booms. Peter Langille, a well-known blacksmith from nearby North-West Cove, had seven sons, five of whom went on to become successful shipwrights. There were seventeen blacksmiths in Lunenburg town ca. 1905: Harry Bailly, William Bailly, Edwin Bailly, Moyle Crouse, Bertrum Dauphinee, George Dauphinee, Gilbert Dauphinee, Henry Dauphinee, Joseph Dauphinee, Roy Dauphinee, George Hamm, Ralph Selig, Irvin Spidle, Urban Spidle, Thomas Walters, Isaiah Wamboldt, and Obediah Wamboldt.

THOMAS WALTER'S BLACKSMITH SHOP, CA. 1900

Thomas Walters began his business in 1893 on this site at the corner of Kempt & Montague Streets. He was followed in later years by his son Johnnie, who is the small boy standing to the left in the photo. The tradition was carried on in turn by his son Vernon Walters, a third generation blacksmith who retired in the early 1990s after many years of being Lunenburg's remaining link to the shipsmiths from the days of sail.

FRANK POWERS PLUMBING & HEATING

Workers pose with two roof-top air circulators built at Frank Powers ca. 1900. Frank Powers (1853-1911) opened his Lunenburg business in 1874 manufacturing

an array of products including mechanical fog alarms, ships' signals, lanterns, bicycles, and hot-water heating apparatus. Annual sales ca. 1894 were $20,000. His claim to fame was the designing and manufacturing of the Bluenose Foghorn which came to be widely used on the Atlantic, West Coast and Great Lakes. Upon his death the business was continued by his sons until its closure in the 1980s.

FRANK POWERS PLUMBING & HEATING

A young woman poses in her riding costume for this early 1900s L.A. Hirtle photo taken at his studio on Lincoln Street. The bicycle may very well have been manufactured at Frank Powers' establishment and purchased from bicycle dealer F.L. McNeil on Duke Street. In 1892, Powers reputedly designed and sold an electric bicycle although to date there have been no details found to confirm this.

S.A. ROUNSEFELL DRUGS & FANCY GOODS

S.A. Rounsefell's was a business fixture on Lincoln Street for fifty years. Featured in this photo are owner and druggist Samuel A. Rounsefell and clerk Florence Burns, ca. 1915. In 1896 Rounsefell's was advertised as an "Importer and Dealer in Drugs, Patent Medicines, Perfumery Toilet Articles, Fancy Goods, Pipes, Tobacco, Cigars. Field, Garden and Flower Seeds in Season."

WOMEN IN THE WORK PLACE

An unidentified lady, possibly a clerk, poses at what appears to be a pharmacy counter in this ca. 1905 photo. Women who worked were generally unmarried and their job opportunities were limited. McAlpine's 1908 Directory listed the following positions as filled by women in Lunenburg town: six stenographers, one typist, one book-keeper, one general clerk, two drug clerks, three school teachers, four dressmakers, one hotel clerk, two telegraph operators, and two telephone operators. Those independently employed were Mrs. A. M. Hammett, Mrs. Tamer Hirtle, and Mrs. Isaac Gates, all proprietors of boarding houses, and Miss Christina Ross who owned a candy store on Duke Street. Some women did not name their profession while fifty-one others were categorized only as widows.

C. Albert Smith's Threshing Mill, Sash, Door & Mouldings Factory

C. Albert Smith operated his mill and factory on Prince Street from 1883 to 1910. Ripened grain was separated from the husk or stalk by a beating action known as threshing. This was done using a hand-held instrument called a flail or a threshing machine such as the one owned by Albert Smith's. The grain was then taken to a grist mill, of which there were fifty-six in Lunenburg County in the mid-1800s, to be ground into flour. Barley was the principle crop grown in the county, yielding 52,085 bushels in 1891 followed by oats (36,900 bushels) and rye (12,246 bushels). Wheat did not grow particularly well, although in the fall of 1883 a Mr. Charles Eikle, of Crousetown, was reported as having produced 18 1/2 bushels on only three-tenths of an acre, using just 12 1/2 quarts of wheat—a return of over fifty-fold.

TANNERY AND WAGON LOADS OF HIDES, CA. 1890

Lunenburg's Tannery Road (once called Tan-yard Road) attests to the importance of tanning hides in the early 1800s. In 1826 Lunenburg was importing hundreds of hides and the census of 1851 lists ten tanneries in the township. Within a decade, however, the number had been cut to four and by 1896 there was only Joseph Risser and Frank Risser on Mahone Bay Road and Philip Rissie on North-West Road advertising their services as tanners.

The drop in businesses was no doubt attributable, to some degree, to the decline of the moose and caribou populations. Moose hides and meat, and to a lesser degree caribou, were highly marketable commodities, especially in Halifax and St. John. Using dogs to run them to exhaustion, or pits and snares to entrap them, both were hunted unmercifully throughout Nova Scotia during the 1800s. In his county history, DesBrisay makes reference to one Lunenburg hunter in a party who "killed and helped to kill fifty-five moose and eight caribou."

With the introduction of game laws, hunting seasons, and wardens by the late 1800s, the moose survived but there has not been a province-wide hunting season since 1937. Caribou, on the other hand, declined through the 1860s, were very scarce in the 1870s and by the early 1900s had become extinct in Nova Scotia.

In McAlpine's 1908 Directory there were no tanners listed for Lunenburg town, but in the county as a whole there were eight-Charles and Hugh Stanford, Benjamin and Douglas Mills at Chester, H.S. and Norman Morton at New Germany, Ernest James at Mahone Bay, and Stanley Hebb in Bridgewater.

LUNENBURG IRON FOUNDRY (4 PHOTOS) Lunenburg Iron Foundry, incorporated in December 1891, was the town's first large-scale manufacturing enterprise. Equipped at the time with "the most improved machinery" and occupying twelve thousand square feet of work space, the foundry turned out cooking and heating stoves, brass and iron ship castings, mill and general machinery and bells weighing from one hundred to seven hundred pounds. Sales exceeded $30,000 annually. Featured here is an early molding room gang, ca. 1910. From left to right: Mr. Emeneau, Arthur Schwartz, Albert Young, Witney Wamboldt, Jimmy Hall, Melburne Myra, Jim Young, Bob Silver, Freeman Corkum, Edwin Therleau, Aubrey Brown, and Lemmy Schwartz.

A major fire at the foundry in 1906 proved nearly fatal but the business was bought and rebuilt by a company spearheaded by John James Kinley.

Pouring Molten Steel, 1940s. During World War Two, five hundred men were employed at Lunenburg Foundry refitting corvettes and other naval vessels.

BARREL MAKING

Three of Lunenburg's traditional trades are featured in this one photo, as rows of barrels and stacks of dories form a backdrop to the unloading of dried fish at dockside. Manufacturing barrels for fish, fish oil, potatoes, apples, flour and nails, as well as wooden boxes for packing and shipping fish, was a major industry in Nova Scotia until the mid-1900s. The 1861 census for Lunenburg County lists among its numerous products: 5,992 barrels of mackerel, 28,665 barrels of herring, 1177 barrels of Gaspereaux, 47,067 gallons of fish oil, 153,954 bushels of potatoes and 200,813 pounds of butter. Six million barrel hoops were produced annually in Nova Scotia with New Ross, Lunenburg County considered the "barrel hoop centre" of the province. As early as the 1830s, barrels from the Ross family mill were being hauled by ox team to Chester Basin and shipped on schooners to the Halifax market. Early Lunenburg coopers, ca. 1871, were Andrew Myrah, William Townsend, Francis and Louis Silver. In 1892 Lunenburg had four coopers listed—Seaboyer & Son, Elias Silver, George Townshend, and Wilbur Sawler. Elias Silver's was the largest of the cooperages with revenues of $11,000 annually. Others who took up the trade were blacksmiths Elvin and Edwin Bailly, Joshua Hirtle, William Emeneau, and Charles Maxner.

The barrel industry continued to flourish into the 1930s when Nova Scotia produced 1,500,000 barrels, as well as 164 million board feet of staves and headings for shipment to the West Indies to make large kegs of molasses. By the 1950s industry demand for barrels had declined significantly in favour of wooden boxes.

RUM-RUNNING

The Fisheries Museum of the Atlantic in Lunenburg has an extensive display concerning the days of Prohibition and rum-running. Featured among the photos, artifacts, and anecdotal information is the story of the rum-runner *Reo II*, pictured here, which until 1985 formed a part of the museum's floating exhibits at dockside. Built in 1931 at Meteghan, Nova Scotia, the vessel spent the first five of her fifty-four years running illicit liquor to the United States. Like many vessels built in the 1930s she was designed specifically for the rum trade. Her low-to-the-water silhouette and drab colour made detection difficult for the Canadian Preventive Service, R.C.M.P., and American Coast Guard all of whom had the job—with little public support—to stem the flow of booze. In contrast to the Chicago gun-toting Capone types of Prohibition, the men who manned the supply vessels were, for the most part, hard-working, otherwise law-abiding individuals who found rum running a well-paying, albeit often dangerous, vocation to support their families. During the Roaring Twenties and Dirty Thirties, "there appeared to be almost as many Lunenburg vessels rum-running as there were fishing." The legalities aside, many communities owed their very survival during the lean years of the Depression to the spiritous trade.

In the early 1900s, Canadian laws pertaining to liquor were split between provincial and federal jurisdictions. Liquor sales were controlled provincially while its manufacture and importing/exporting was federally controlled. Prohibition—which made it illegal to manufacture, sell, or transport liquor—was, in a general context, effective in parts of the United States and Canada between 1916-1948. The entire United States was declared "dry" between 1920-1933 while in Canada a nation-wide ban was much shorter, lasting from 1916 to1919, after which individual provinces once again became 'wet'—Quebec, British Columbia, Yukon in 1921; Manitoba in 1923; Alberta in 1924; Saskatchewan in 1925; Ontario, New Brunswick in 1927, Nova Scotia in 1930, and Prince Edward Island, much later, in 1948. While Canadian distillers were still allowed, under federal laws, to export their products during this time, they could not export to nations enforcing Prohibition. In other words the lucrative U.S. market was closed to them. To circumvent the legalities, the French-owned islands of St. Pierre and Miquelon off the Canadian coast became a focal point for sales. Acting as a "clearing house" more than one thousand vessels loaded up with liquor in St. Pierre alone and made the rum-run to the U.S. coast. Most times, they anchored safely outside the twelve-mile limit in international waters and off-loaded their contraband, as featured in this photo, onto speed boats for the run to shore. Lunenburg native Hugh Corkum wrote an entertaining and informative book, *On Both Sides of the Law*, of his ten-year stint in the rum-trade. As the book's title suggests he then became ironically the town's long-serving police chief.

RUM-RUNNER, NARMADA

Here, the rum-runner *Narmada* is at dockside in Lunenburg. Not all rum-runners were sleek, steel-plated, powerboats. Many were two- and three-masted fishing schooners that were sold into the trade by owners answering advertisements involving cash sales for "seaworthy vessels."

Prohibition was not an early twentieth century phenomenon. In 1878, the Canadian Temperance Act was passed, effectively signalling the start of Prohibition. Until 1900, however, it was not actively enforced; individual communities were allowed to vote regularly on being 'wet' or 'dry.' At the forefront of these votes were the temperance societies; one of the first in Lunenburg County was organized in about 1826 in Bridgewater. Through the efforts of the Lodges of British Templars, Independent Order of Good Templars, Loyal Temperance Legion, and Women's Christian Temperance Union it was reported in 1895, albeit somewhat optimistically, that "one of the greatest blessings to the county has been the spread of total abstinence." Such was not the case, of course, as "free use of intoxicating liquor" was an accepted part of barn raisings, breaking frolics, hauling parties, battalion days, in-session court days and, naturally, elections—to "drink was fashionable."

Public Service

Town Utilities

Looking east on Lincoln Street, showing north side between Cornwallis and Duke Streets, featuring C.C. Morash's tailor shop, a photograph gallery, and Wah Hop Chinese Laundry ca. 1910. This photo is interesting in that it depicts the town's electric and telephone utilities and a road crew working on repairs to the street or possibly the water system. Prior to incorporation in 1888, Lunenburg had telephone lines installed to fifty customers and the Maritimes' first incandescent lighting plant had been built by E.L. Nash. Its water works, however, lagged behind other towns as the majority of older residents believed that traditional means of wells and gathering rain water were adequate. It was a hotly debated issue among ratepayers throughout the 1880s until, finally in 1893, by the slimmest of a twelve-vote majority, Lunenburg began work on a modern water conveyance system.

LUNENBURG'S FIRST CHURCH St. John's Anglican Church dates from 1754 and is the second oldest Anglican church in Canada, after St. Paul's in Halifax. The building materials were imported from Boston because at the time there was no mill in Nova Scotia capable of producing the sawed timbers. Until the 1770s, St. John's was the only church in Lunenburg and was shared by the Anglican, Presbyterian, and Lutheran congregations. While the original structure has never been replaced—its oak frame long rumoured to have come from Boston's old King's Chapel—St. John's, featured here ca. 1900, underwent a number of significant Gothic alterations by Lunenburg shipwrights and master carpenters in 1840, again between 1870 and 1875, and finally in 1892. The western European style of Gothic architecture traditionally featured the pointed arch, the flying butress, and extensive ornamentation. Terry James and Bill Plaskett's *Buildings of Old Lunenburg* describes the church today as "one of the most striking early wooden churches in the country and perhaps the very best example of the 'Carpenter Gothic' style...and it sits like a serene jewel in the centre of the Old Town."

St. Andrew's Presbyterian Church, ca. late 1800s
The oldest Presbyterian congregation in Canada originated in Lunenburg from the early founding Calvinists or Reformed Protestants, who first held worship services outside, or in, members' homes. In 1759, arrangements were made to use St. John's Anglican Church and the congregation used the church until 1770 when construction was completed on their own house of worship.

Its first minister, Reverend Bruin Romkes Comingoe, served the congregation for fifty years until his death in 1820. The original church was replaced in 1828 and named St. Andrew's sometime during the pastorate of Reverend William Duff (1843–1880). The church underwent a major change in 1879 when it was expanded in size, its spire raised to 118 feet, and stained glass Gothic windows installed. For many years, married and unmarried parishioners were segregated to opposite sides of the church. Women sat on the ground floor pews, men in the gallery, elders, and deacons to either side of the pulpit. The building seen here to the left was rented out by the church in the 1850s to a Miss Gow who taught school in two of the ground-floor rooms.

**ZION'S
EVANGELICAL
LUTHERAN
CHURCH**

Zion's Evangelical Lutheran Church, like St. Andrew's Presbyterian, boasts the oldest congregation in Canada. Originally holding outdoor services, and then sharing St. John's Anglican Church, the first Lutheran church was built in 1770 by volunteer labour, with a popular legend claiming that it was fortified with eleven gallons of rum and twenty gallons of spruce beer. Charles Ernest Cossmann became its fourth minister in 1835 and served forty-one years until retiring in 1876, at which time he had baptized 3,966 persons, married 622 couples, buried 1,041 corpses, and preached 11,000 sermons. During his ministry, he travelled four thousand miles a year by horseback, preaching in German throughout Lunenburg, Queens, and Halifax Counties. He is credited with the establishment of Lutheran parishes in Bridgewater and Mahone Bay. The original Lunenburg church was replaced in 1841 and again in 1890 when it was designed in the "High Victorian Gothic" style pictured here.

A beautiful stained glass window in the south wall is dedicated to the memory of Reverend Cossmann who died in 1897 at the age of ninety-one. One of the many artifacts contained in the church today is the Antoine-Marie Bell. Possessing a storied history, it was one of three bells given as a gift to Louisbourg in 1735 by Louis XV of France. With the fall of the fortress in 1758, the bell was taken to Halifax where it remained until 1776 when purchased by the Lunenburg Lutherans. When American privateers sacked the town in 1782, the bell was unceremoniously dumped into Back Harbour but was subsequently rescued and returned to the belfry. In 1972 it was placed in the sanctuary during celebrations of the church's bicentennial.

CENTRAL UNITED CHURCH

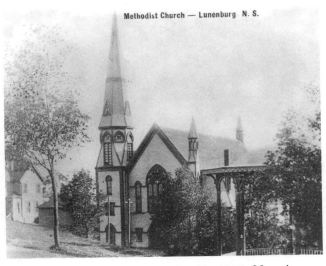

Methodist Church — Lunenburg N. S.

In 1812, George Orth, one of four Lunenburg men ex-communicated by the Lutheran Church for conducting prayer meetings in opposition to Lutheran doctrines, began a ministry for those of a similar faith. A year later Orth and thirty Methodist parishioners built a small church near the town's Parade Square. Measuring only thirty by forty feet, it was cut in half and ten feet were added to the middle of the building in 1865; in 1871 an additional twenty-foot extension was built on the north end. Work began on a new, larger church (pictured here) in 1883 and when completed in 1885, fifteen hundred people attended the dedication service. In 1928, a majority of Canadian Presbyterians and Congregational Churches joined with the Methodists (St. Andrew's abstained) to form the United Church of Canada. While the church may not be the oldest in Lunenburg it is said to be the largest, measuring fifty-six by one-hundred and twelve feet.

FIRST ACADEMY

A rare photo of Lunenburg's first Academy ca. 1865. Religious orders were generally responsible for early education, holding classes in churches, public buildings, or family homes if a school was not available. A petition for Lunenburg's first government-supported school master was made in 1762. An act was passed in 1811 establishing grammar schools in several counties including Lunenburg; in 1826 a meeting was held in the town's court house to organize a district school. Until the Free School Act in 1864 parents were expected to pay for their children's education; for those less fortunate Lunenburg had four schools for poor children supported by "private subscription." With free schooling, the decision was made in 1864 to build an Academy on the town's Parade. Completed in 1865, it measured fifty by ninety feet with a fifty-foot 'L'-shape, the four classrooms inside housed more than two hundred students. The Academy was later enlarged to eight or ten rooms with a second storey addition. On September 28, 1893, with school in session, a fire razed the building without injury or loss of life.

LUNENBURG ACADEMY CA 1900

After the loss of the town's first academy in 1893, a second was built a year later on Gallows Hill. Observers at the time boasted that it was to be the "best-equipped institution of its kind in Nova Scotia."

Without question, the new academy had the best of everything. Its twelve classrooms were connected to the principal's office with individual electric bells and speaking tubes. Each pupil had their own desk and access to a library, laboratory, cloakrooms, and an assembly hall with seating for more than four hundred. Six furnaces gave classrooms "a constant supply of pure warm air" circulated from the outside. A six-hundred-pound bell in one of the towers signalled the start of school; students entered through six entrances, "affording a complete separation of boys from girls except in the classroom." The interior was finished in birch and ash "giving to the whole a substantial and neat appearance."

Completed in 1895, at a cost of thirty thousand dollars, it stands today as Lunenburg's most prominent landmark and the only academy building that remains in Nova Scotia from the nineteenth century.

MANUAL TRAINING CLASS

An interesting late-1800s photo taken at the academy depicts a manual training class. The age of the participants suggests they may have been teachers receiving specialized instruction or possibly an adult education class. The Census of 1891 reported that out of a population of 31,075 living in Lunenburg County, 19,782 could read and write, 2,439 could read, and 8,854 were illiterate. By 1895 there were 180 teachers in the county, the total expenditure on salaries for the year, without provincial grants, amounted to $15,690. Thirty-four teachers had received training at Normal College in Truro. There were 171 schools and "every settlement has now its public school, and every one of the 146 sections is organized and active." Total enrollment for the county was 7,552 students-3,915 boys and 3,637 girls. John Thomas who died in 1881, at age eighty-three, and taught throughout the county, provided a footnote about the improvements to Lunenburg's educational system. Upon his retirement, he received the teacher's bonus of one hundred-acres of forestland, "the special provincial acknowledgment for long service in the education of the young." Reminiscing about his early experiences as a teacher, he commented:

> You are aware that teachers at the present day are more cared for than teachers formerly. I have in some sections had for food, in poor families where I boarded, nothing but Indian meal, without milk or sweetening ... slept on hay and straw beds on the floor where mice, fleas, and bugs could be felt all hours of the night. I have frequently found one, two or three mice crushed to death lying under me—the straw not even put in a sack, and my covering old clothing. I suffered all this, so great was my wish to give instruction to the poor and rising generation. Yea, many families of poor children have I educated and never received one farthing.

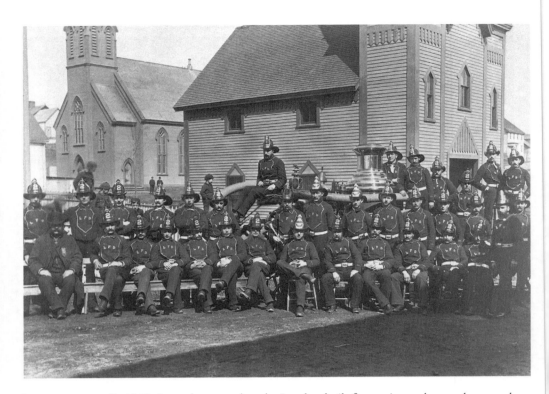

LUNENBURG FIRE DEPARTMENT VOLUNTEERS

In 1819, Lunenburg purchased a London-built fire engine and a year later a volunteer fire company was formed. Its first captain was Casper Oxner, followed in succession by George Anderson, Lewis Anderson, John Dauphinee, Michael Anderson, and Henry Dauphinee. On April 19, 1838 the Lunenburg Crown Fire Company was organized with thirty-two members. President was Geo. T. Solomon, Vice-President Chas. J. Rudolph, and Secretary-Treasurer Daniel Owen. DesBrisay's county history mentions another un-named fire department for Lunenburg in 1876 which may have been a completely re-structured one, or a separate branch of the Crown Fire Company, perhaps an axe and ladder division. In 1885, a steam fire-engine was bought from Brussels, Ontario after a volunteer fireman died fighting a blaze. An advertisement was also run that year seeking additional volunteers; all twenty-six who applied were accepted.

CENTRAL FIRE STATION CA. 1900

The highlight for fire protection in Lunenburg would appear to have come in 1889 with the completion of a new engine house. "Besides the room for the engine and appliances, it has a handsome parlour and other convenient rooms, the floor of one being polished ash. The whole establishment reflects the highest credit on the Lunenburg firemen, and all who aided them in the work."

POSTAL SERVICE

In 1893, Lunenburg's small, outdated post office on Lincoln Street (above, ca. 1880), was replaced by this new federal postal and customs building on King Street. DesBrisay writes that the earliest postal deliveries were carried once a week by John Vienot on horseback between Lunenburg and Bridgewater. In 1757, the first road was cut between Halifax and Lunenburg. Mail from Halifax to Liverpool travelled via Lunenburg and the LaHave Ferry where a James Nicholson operated a scow. This postal route was discontinued in the mid-1800s when a road was cut from Mahone Bay to Bridgewater, then extended to Mill Village, Queens County. Two of Lunenburg's earliest, long-serving postmasters/mistresses were the Hon.William Rudolf (1791-1859) and his wife Anna Matilda Oxner (1810-1886). William Rudolf, whose grandfather Leonard Christopher Rudolf was the second proprietor, named in the original Lunenburg grant, held a number of public offices during his lifetime including seats in the House of Assembly and Legislative Council, Justice of the Peace and Registrar of Deeds. He was also a Lieutenant-Colonel of 1st Battalion Lunenburg and a long-time West Indies merchant in the firm William Rudolf & Co.

Federal postal and customs building

COURT HOUSE / TOWN HALL, 1890s

Lunenburg's first court house was erected in 1775 and it was reported in the *History of Lunenburg County* that "to their honor, they are said to settle a great part of their matters by arbitration. The judges are careful to advise them to settle their matters in an amicable manner, which sometimes hath the desired effect. The cases before the court are but few...though some are obliged to make use of the law in their own defence." The town's first jail, a stone building known as the "King's Prison," was built in 1753; a new lock-up replaced it in 1816. The office of High Sheriff was responsible for keeping law and order. Philip Knaut was appointed to the position at the time of the town's founding; he also served as coroner, Justice of the Peace, owned one of the earliest stores, and represented the county in the first Nova Scotia Parliament. Knaut was succeeded as sheriff by his son, Benjamin, who was followed by William Dalton in 1784, then Edward James in 1788. Henry Kaulbach took office in 1798, serving until 1828 when his son John assumed the position, carrying on the family tradition for another fifty years until he retired a year before his death at the age of eighty-two.

By 1890, the jail and court house were in need of repairs and plans were made for the new building featured here to house both facilities. The cornerstone was laid in 1891 and when work finished in 1893 it contained the law court, public offices, a three cell jail, and a gallows that was never used. At the time, much controversy surrounded its construction because Lunenburg and Bridgewater were both vying to be the county seat for the proposed courthouse. Before any decision could be reached as to its location, the two towns went ahead with building their own which led, in 1893, to a special act of legislation. The "Act to Settle Difficulties That Have Arisen With Regard to the Courthouse in the County of Lunenburg" was primarily a compromise that alternated court sessions between the rival communities.

Chapter 5

Life at Sea

SUPERSTITIONS

Centuries-old mariner superstitions are common throughout Nova Scotia sea ports; some have Lunenburg-Germanic origins while many are shared among a variety of nationalities and counties. An interesting feature of this unique photo—depicting an emergency sewing repair to a rip in the mainsail canvas—is the color of the fisherman's mittens. A widely held belief was that only white mittens should be worn aboard ships—grey or red brought bad luck. Either the crew of this vessel did not ascribe to such tales or this particular pair had been darkened from continual exposure to the elements and shipboard duties. Other omens of good and bad fortune rooted in Lunenburg folklore included uttering the word "pig" aboard a fishing vessel which was believed was sure to bring an ill wind; as a sign of good luck a vessel, when launched, needed to slip off the ways and turn to seaward; sticking a knife in the spar would bring wind to a becalmed vessel; a ship would go bottom-up if a loaf of bread turned upside down during the voyage; woodshavings on deck were bad luck and had to be quickly swept away (but there can be no sweeping after six o'clock or misfortune would follow regardless); a sailor when boarding a vessel must step 'just so' or he won't sail; sailing on the thirteenth of a month, launching a ship on Friday, hammering a nail on-board a vessel on Sunday, or loading supplies from the eastern side of a wharf were all certain harbingers of bad things to come.

**"LORD, ERE WE GO, TO THEE WE TRUST OUR ALL,
THY SEA IS MIGHTY, AND OUR BOATS ARE SMALL."**

—FISHERMEN'S PRAYER

The Fishermen's Memorial in Lunenburg contains the names of 128 vessels lost at sea, forty-one of which went down with all hands. Inscribed alongside are the names of the 692 mariners, "who have gone down to the sea in ships and who have never returned."

John P. Parker writes in *Sails of the Maritimes*: "The majority of the schooners met what may be described as a 'violent end' and very few died in bed of old age. Many went down in heavy weather from the loss of sails, rudders and spars; hulls opened up and hatches staved in. Many literally 'vanished' while many others were classed as 'abandoned at sea.'" *Bluenose* skipper Angus Walters once said: "There were times when a little religion was mighty handy. The fo'c's'le is a damned poor place for an atheist because he'd find little company."

REEFING THE MAINSAIL

The crew of a fishing schooner is called out to reef the mainsail. A fisherman needed always to be vigilant when the spectre of death or serious injury was ever-present from continual exposure to the mercies of the sea. A careless slip, an errant boom, or a rogue wave could plunge a body into frigid waters from which there was little hope of rescue. Fishermen were notorious for not knowing how to swim, their argument being they were too busy fishing to learn.

There is a story of a Lunenburg cook who was swept unexpectedly overboard during rough weather. Putting out the dories, the crew searched in vain for the doomed non-swimmer. Finding only his bowler hat floating on the surface, a saddened doryman reached over to retrieve it as a family momento. To his surprise, the cook was still attached, and after a few minutes of resuscitation, he lived to sail again.

WORKING THE "WIDOW MAKER"

Three fishermen clad in foul weather gear balance precariously as they struggle "to make the jib fast," ca 1912. The jib was a triangular headsail rigged from the foremast to the bowsprit, the large spar that projected beyond the bow of a vessel. Such work was extremely dangerous lending the nickname of 'widow maker' to the bowsprit because so many men were lost while working from there in bad weather. T.E. McManus of Boston did away with it in about 1901 when he designed a schooner with the bow projected forward in a long over-hang. The new vessel, known as a "knockabout" lessened the inherent dangers and increased the ship's maneuverability around wharves. While more expensive to build, knockabouts became very popular especially when engines were first installed in the early 1900s. The first knockabout to be built at Lunenburg was the *General Haig* in 1918 by Smith & Rhuland, the last being the *Jean Frances* in 1949.

SETTING THE TOPSAIL

A schooner's penant flutters high above the main deck while a crew member sets the topsail, ca. 1913. A vessel usually flew a pennant with its name inscribed as well as the customary 'Red Duster' flag. Tradition called for a lowering of the flag to half-mast when someone had died during the voyage. The following lines from a poem in DesBrisay's county history leaves one imagining the dread a waiting wife or mother would have suffered as their loved one's vessel hove into sight of the harbour approaches with its flag lowered: *Half-mast high the signal floats! She's coming in from sea. Some sailor of her crew is gone—Who may the lost one be?*

**HANDLINING
CA. 1910**

Until the late 1800s, handlining from the deck of an anchored vessel was the principal method used when fishing cod and other ground fish off the Labrador and Nova Scotia coasts. Lines reaching depths of fifty to one hundred feet and more were dropped over the side, each line having a heavy lead sinker and one or two hooks generally baited with mackerel, herring, squid, or capelin. Jigging and hauling in fish was a chore the fisherman could expect to repeat 350 times in the course of a day's work. Vessels sailing to Labrador would also carry two or three large open boats called whalers for use when fishing in sight of land, the general rule being, one whaler for every thirty tons of vessel weight. Propelled with oars or a sail, two men to a boat would handline for cod up to three miles from the schooner and were expected to catch two-boat loads a day, weather permitting. By the early 1870s, the cumbersome whaler and restrictive nature of handlining from an anchored schooner gave way to the more efficient, flat-bottomed Gloucester dory and trawl fishing.

BEGINNINGS OF DORY FISHING

It is thought that Lunenburg fishermen first began using dories in the 1870s, no doubt having been introduced to them by the U.S. Gloucester fleet which, according to some, had been fishing from these crafts since the 1850s. Dories were one of the most sea-worthy of small boats and, by their design, could be stacked easily or 'nested' on a vessel's deck by removing the thwarts. They were also better suited to hauling trawl lines than the whaler or Labrador boats and allowed for a much greater area to be covered when handlining than vessel fishing. Dories were outfitted with oars and a sail and generally painted a yellow-orange for better visibility in fog, snow, or at dusk when the not uncommon experience of missing the safe haven of a schooner could result, at the very least, in a night adrift on the North Atlantic. Each dory carried an array of equipment marked with the number of that particular boat including anchors, two or three buoys made from small kegs, markers, bailers, kerosene flare, water and food, compass, gaff, club, a bait tub, and as many as four trawl tubs.

NESTS OF DORIES

TOP RIGHT

Crew members work at shipboard duties amidst nests of dories. Lunenburg dories were generally of two sizes: single dories twelve feet in length (measured along the boat's bottom) and two-man dories, fifteen-feet bottom measure. The number carried was determined by the type of fishing to be done. Vessels handlining would have fifteen to twenty-one single dories while those outfitted for trawl fishing used six to twelve double dories. With onboard space at a premium, stacking dories kept them efficiently stored out of the way until needed when they could be easily swung out and lowered. Lunenburg fishermen tell stories of their hands worked raw and numb from hauling trawl lines when after a day of fishing, it took six men to lift one end of a dory.

BAITING UP THE TRAWLS

BOTTOM RIGHT

Baiting trawl lines was time-consuming work generally done below decks in the early morning hours before heading out for a day of dory fishing. Trawls were more expensive to fish than handlines because they required far greater quantities of bait, and it had to be fresh as cod were not attracted to salted bait.

NESTS OF DORIES

BAITING UP THE TRAWLS

One man rows a dory amid tubs of trawl while his partner coils line, ca. 1914. Lunenburg fishermen began fishing trawls (also known as longlining) in the 1870s although they were possibly used as early as the 1860s in some parts of southwestern Nova Scotia and the United States. A trawl was a one- or one-and-a-half-mile length of sturdy tarred cotton line from which shorter lines of two or three feet called ganglings were strung every three feet with a single hook. The trawl or ground line was made up of individual lengths called 'shots' measuring fifty fathoms (three hundred feet). Seven 'shots' were normally bent together and coiled in a trawl tub, it taking four tubs to make up a one-and-a-half mile trawl.

The trawl was laid while one man rowed and the other threw out an anchor and marker buoy to which the ground line was attached, then let the rest of the line out with a 'heaving stick' until reaching the end of the trawl when another anchor and marker buoy went over the side. A marker buoy might also be placed at the midway point of the trawl. The men then smoked or returned to the schooner for a hot drink while waiting for the fish to bite. A few hours later, the trawl would be pulled into the dory, the catch removed, hooks rebaited, and the trawl re-set. A fish every fifteen hooks was considered a reasonable catch.

The "setting and hauling" of trawls was soon replaced with a more efficient method known as "underrunning" (pioneered by Capt. Ben Anderson of Lunenburg in 1873), whereby the trawl remained set while the dory worked up and down its length with part of the trawl always laying across the dory. One man would pull the fish onboard, unhook and drop them into the dory's bottom while the other rebaited each gangling and dropped it over the side. This was a much more efficient method and it was possible to repeat the procedure three or four times in the run of a day.

LOADING FRESH BAIT IN NEWFOUND-LAND

Schooners generally carried an initial supply of fresh bait with them to the fishing banks, sometimes packing it in ice. When this was depleted or spoiled, it was necessary to replenish stocks from inshore fishermen or catch their own. Much fishing time could be wasted from frequent trips to coastal outports. The Magdalen Islands with large numbers of capelin were a favorite spot for bait, especially near the end of the spring trip or the start of the summer season. With nearly a thousand fishing schooners from Nova Scotia, Gloucester, and Newfoundland all vying for fresh bait, there were seasons when bait prices doubled or tripled, and worse yet, when supply could not keep up with demand, resulting in severe economic losses for the season.

HANDLINING REMAINED POPULAR

A doryman usually worked two handlines at the same time, tying one off when a fish was hooked. While trawl fishing gained wide spread usage among the Lunenburg fleet in the late 1800s, handlining from dories remained a viable alternative, the LaHave in Lunenburg County especially noted for this method. Handlining was at a disadvantage in that it matched one hook against eighteen hundred on a mile-length of trawl. However, handlining usually attracted only larger fish and there was less bait wastage from nibbling than occurred with the bottom-laid trawl line. A report for 1888 revealed that the first arrival in Lunenburg from that summer's fishing expedition was the handline schooner *J.A. Hirtle*. Its Captain Geldert boasted they had caught one thousand quintals (112,000 pounds) of fish big enough that sixty of which would load a dory.

A hard-working and lucky handlining crew could wind up as the "highliner" of the fleet, the title bestowed upon the schooner having the largest catch of the season.

FLYING SETS

TOP RIGHT

When a schooner reached the fishing banks, it anchored and the dories dispersed at the captain's orders in a pattern similar to that of spokes from a wheel's hub. An alternate method was the flying set pictured here, ca. 1910. Dories were lowered and towed astern in two lines while the schooner moved slowly along a designated course. Each dory would be cast off at half-mile intervals to begin their day of fishing. The schooner would then anchor and wait for the dories to return with their catch. Note the numbered marker buoy that would be dropped when setting the trawl line. Fishermen went out in all manner of weather and trying to locate these markers a mile or more from the schooner in darkness, rain, snow, or fog on the expanse of the North Atlantic was no mean feat. Using a compass and allowing for tides and wind, dorymen often counted oar strokes as a way of relocating their trawl after unloading a catch of fish. If they missed the mark, the dory had to be rowed back to the vessel, against all elements, and the procedure started again until the trawl was found, sometimes taking hours away from valuable fishing time.

APPLYING THE 'FISH KILLER'

A doryman prepares to subdue a halibut with his 'fish killer,' a small club sometimes called a 'priest' or 'gob.' While cod was the most valuable species, others like haddock, pollock, and hake would be salted and packed together in the hold. Halibut was iced if possible and marketed fresh upon returning to port.

Cod averaged five pounds in weight, the record weighing two hundred; a sixty-pound cod however was certainly not uncommon at that time. Cod are not a fighting fish and can be hauled virtually limp into the dory.

Such is not the case with halibut. A 'gurdy' or hand-winch was often used to bring these behemoths to the surface and unlike cod they did not come willingly, usually being quite 'lively' when hooked. Halibut averaged fifty pounds, the record tipping the scales at seven hundred pounds and measuring seven feet-long. The fish would be clubbed before being pulled into the dory and lashed down, just in case the *coup de grâce* had been but a stunning blow. The North Atlantic in a seventeen-foot dory was not the place to be with a suddenly very much alive two hundred pound fish.

PRESERVING THE CATCH It was imperative to clean and salt the day's catch as soon as possible in order to prevent spoilage. When a dory came alongside, the fish were forked onto the schooner's deck, then pitched onto work tables called "keds" or "keelers" to be handled by the "dressing crew." The 'throater' cut the fish's throat, saved the tongues, and split it part way, before the 'header' removed the head and entrails, saving the liver for oil. The 'splitter' finished the job, removed the backbone and flattened the fish, then soaked it clean in a tub of saltwater. The 'salter' then took charge of salting and storing the catch in the hold. A Lunenburg schooner used on average fifteen hogsheads (140 bushels) of salt for every 100 quintals (11,200 pounds) of fish.

The salter's job was crucial because the piles, or kenches, of cod were heavily salted between layers and care had to be taken not to leave hollows where the pickle would collect and redden the fish, thereby diminishing its market value. A well-salted catch could be kept for long periods before curing which was important when trips to the Grand Banks off Newfoundland lasted for three months.

FISHING WAS A COOPERATIVE BUSINESS

"The accounts of a fishing trip were settled on a co-operative basis between the vessel's owners and crew," explains B.A. Balcom in his book *History of the Lunenburg Fishing Industry*. The captain's commission (usually two-and-a-half per cent), the header's and throater's wages, the cost of bait and ice, and the charges for fish making and delivery were all deducted from the gross returns. The remainder was divided equally between the owners and crew. The owners were responsible for paying the major costs of outfitting, including provisions, salt, and fishing gear. After these charges were met, the owner's portion was divided and issued as dividends on the shares. The crew paid the cook's wages, marine insurance, and other costs incidental to the voyage from their portion before dividing it into shares. Crews working on shares were supposed to be more efficient than those working for wages, but profits were essentially determined by conditions on the fishing grounds and in Lunenburg's export markets:

> With the exception of the header, throater, and cook all of the crew worked on shares. The salter and the captain, in addition to a commission, were each entitled to a share. There were three methods of dividing the shares-equally, 'on count', and by weight. The latter two methods proportioned the shares according to the productivity of the individual dory crews, either by the total number of their catch or by its weight. 'Equal shares' was the simplest procedure but required that the crew members be known to be good workers. If their work ethic was unknown, then the proportional method was favoured by the captain on the theory it made the crew more industrious. As the 'on count' method was open to abuse by fishermen throwing the more valuable large fish overboard to make room in their dory for more small fish, weight was sometimes used as the basis for proportioning shares.

"The fishermen took enormous pride in their ability to withstand danger and discomfort and to take them in stride," writes Feenie Ziner in *Bluenose: Queen of the Grand Bank*. "On the saltbanker *Mary L. McKay*, a boarding sea crashed through a half-opened hatch, putting out the fire in the galley stove and flooding the forecastle. The ship keeled over on her beam-ends, pitching men from their bunks, hurling pots, pans, pitchers, plates, and potatoes across the galley. The bosun fought to get down the companionway, both his trouser legs ripped off by the wind. The cook gripped the railing above his stove as boxes, tools, mittens, and pillows surged against his knees. Peering through the clouds of steam from his hissing stove, he inquired, "Hey, Charlie, how's the weather?"

On a more sombre note, the inherent risks associated with a life of fishing are starkly portrayed in the tragic loses suffered by the town of Lunenburg in the gales of 1926 and 1927. While fishing the banks off Sable Island in August 1926, the schooners *Sylvia Mosher* and *Sadie A. Knickle* were caught in a hurricane and went down with all fifty hands. A year later to the month, the Lunenburg and Gloucester fleets were again trapped off Sable Island during the hurricane season. The Lunenburg schooner *Uda R. Corkum*, (pictured here in 1921 during happier times in the eliminations for the International Fishermen's Races), was lost along with three sister ships, the *Clayton Walters*, *Joyce M. Smith* and *Mahala*, taking with them more than eighty fishermen. Within twelve months the Graveyard of the Atlantic had claimed 138 souls.

SCHOONER *UDA R. CORKUM*, LOST IN THE GALE OF 1927

SCHOONER *SADIE A. KNICKLE*, LOST WITH ALL HANDS IN THE GALE OF 1926

DORY FISHING WAS "A FEARFUL DISGUSTIN' JOB"

A popular saying used to go as follows: "A man who would go fishing for a living would go to hell for a pastime." Work hours were long and sleep precious when dropped over a vessel's side at four o'clock in the morning. The day didn't end either when the last dory returned at night. All hands would help the dressing crew with the day's catch, then repair gear and take their turn standing watch. If lucky, a couple of hours rest in the bunk could be had before being called out again to bait trawls and eat breakfast at two or three o'clock in the morning. When the fish were running, it was not unheard of for a crew to go three days with next to no rest, literally falling asleep while standing at the dressing tables with splitting knife in hand. For this a man was paid one, or if really fortunate, one-and-a-half cents a pound for his catch.

Sunday was a day of rest, a time to sleep, wash up, and shave off the week's growth of whiskers. The singing of hymns accompanied by a violin or accordion was a popular form of afternoon entertainment followed by the cook's special meal, roasted salt meat perhaps and a frosted cake.

WARTIME HAZARDS

Lunenburg crews who manned the salt bankers and trading vessels faced dangers on a daily basis from the forces of nature. Their profession became even more hazardous in times of war.

In 1917 Germany sent submarines to the North American eastern seaboard in an effort to disrupt the flow of supplies to Great Britain. Submarine warfare was then in its infancy and even though a number of freighters and fishing vessels were sunk, their effect was only minimal. Lunenburg escaped the U-boat threat until the closing days of World War One when nine fishing schooners sank in August 1918 off Newfoundland. The last of these was the *Elsie Porter* whose crew spent five days in open dories before reaching St. John's.

Again in World War Two, German U-boats attacked the North American east coast, only this time the results were devastating. In a six-month period alone in 1942, five hundred Allied vessels from Newfoundland to the Caribbean were destroyed. One of these was the four-masted Lunenburg schooner *James E. Newsom* pictured here. Well past the days of sail she occupied herself in the coasting trade. The crew consisted of master John R. Wilkie, mate Herbert Stevens, bosun Allan Cross, cook Robert Mosher, and A.B.s Arthur Rhodenizer, Arnold Lohnes, Wilfred Langille, John Allan and Eugene Wilkie.

On May 1, 1942 the *James E. Newsom* was sunk by U-boat shellfire on a voyage from Bridgetown, Barbados to St. John's, Newfoundland while carrying a full cargo of molasses. The crew escaped harm and spent six days in a lifeboat sailing and rowing 250 miles to Bermuda, using only Capt. Wilkie's knowledge of the waters and a sextant to navigate safely.

Chapter 6

The Bluenose

A LEGEND IS BORN

Amid much pomp and circumstance, hundreds gathered on March 26, 1921 to witness the launching of the *Bluenose* from the Smith & Rhuland shipyards. Almost entirely constructed of Nova Scotia wood, with an overall length of 161 feet and a ten-storey high main mast of over 125 feet, *Bluenose* carried a total sail area of 11,139 square feet. Built to race, she also had to be a working salt banker, capturing the high-liner mantle and setting a record for size of catch landed at Lunenburg in the 1920s on her maiden voyage to the Grand Banks. She was "a fisherman deluxe" according to one source, wired throughout with an electrical system, the captain's cabin featuring a brass bed, electricity, and alarms, the crews' quarters being "spacious and second to none in the fleet." Why *Bluenose* dominated her opponents during nearly two decades of racing was debated for years after. Some attributed her success to being built in the open rather than confined to a shed when a severe frost in the spring of 1921 had "set her timbers." Others credited her designer, Bill Roue, or the crews who manned her. In a similar vein, Capt. Angus Walters, who knew *Bluenose* best, believed "it was the way her spars were stepped. If the rest of her is good, a vessel's spars will pretty well tell what she'll do. Somehow, the *Bluenose's* spars was stepped mathematically perfect, in a way that no man could do. I think that was it. I don't feel as there was a vessel that ever came out of Lunenburg that had her sticks stepped that perfect."

**BLUENOSE CA. 1921, QUEEN OF THE NORTH
ATLANTIC FISHERMEN'S INTERNATIONAL RACES**

The inaugural America's Cup Race between Britain and the United States was held in 1851 off the Isle of Wight and featured racing yachts designed specifically for the competition. The United States entry, *America,* won the sixty-mile race and although the British spent an estimated seventy-five million dollars on hull designs in numerous attempts after to wrestle the cup away, they were never successful. Over the years, the men who crewed the Grand Banks schooners came to view the America's Cup with disdain, claiming it wasn't a true test of seamanship. Derisive howls were heard in 1919 when a race was postponed because officials felt twenty-five-knot winds, considered a mere breeze in Lunenburg, posed a danger to participants. Fishing captains from Lunenburg and Gloucester routinely faced off in friendly races on homeward trips from the banks and interest grew in pitting the best of the Canadian and American fleets in an official international contest. In 1920, newspaperman William Dennis announced in the *Halifax Herald* that a series of elimination races would be held in Halifax and Gloucester, the winners to meet in a best-of three challenge match for a cash prize and the Halifax Herald's International Fishermen's Trophy. It was a race that would captivate the Canadian and American public for the next eighteen years.

On October 11, 1920 the *Delawana, Gilbert B. Walters, Alcala, Mona Marie, Bernice Zinck, Freda M. Himmelman, Ruby L. Pentz,* and *Independence* arrived off Point Pleasant Park in Halifax Harbour to determine the Canadian representative for the first North Atlantic Fishermen's International Race. A prerequisite to competing was that a vessel be a working salt banker with at least one full season of experience fishing the Grand Banks.

The *Gilbert B. Walters,* her crew and others featured here at the 1920 elimination races, had no difficulty meeting that criteria, having landed 790,000 pounds of fish the previous season. With her legendary skipper at the helm, (Captain Angus Walters standing to left in third row), the *Gilbert B. Walters* was a pre-race favourite but Delawana carried the day when the *Gilbert B.* broke her fore-topmast and finished five minutes after the first place time.

The American challenger *Esperanto* from Gloucester Massachusetts, skippered by Marty Welch, a 'whitewashed Yankee' originally from Digby, Nova Scotia, made short work of the Delawana in the first international race off Halifax October 30–November 1, 1920. Winning the best of three-race match in two straight she sailed home with four thousand dollars and the Halifax Herald Trophy, leaving a stunned nation in her wake.

The Bluenose Schooner Company, a consortium of business-men headed by Capt. Angus Walters, immediately made plans in 1920 to build a challenger capable of returning the Halifax Trophy to its rightful place the following year. They turned to Bill Roue, whose father James owned a family soft drink bottling company in Halifax dating to 1851, and claimed to be one of the first companies to produce Canadian ginger ale. From an early age, Bill had shown an affinity for building model boats and by the age of twenty-eight had gained a reputation as a naval architect by designing a sailing yacht for the Royal Nova Scotia Yacht Squadron. When approached by the Bluenose Schooner Committee he accepted the job, working on the plans at night through the autumn of 1920 while still employed days at the family bottling factory.

In the meantime, Angus Walters, who owned controlling shares in the new vessel was named her captain, Zwicker & Company were appointed agents and Smith & Rhuland Shipyards in Lunenburg were awarded the contract to build Roue Plan #17. All was completed, from drawing board to christening within five months. Shares were sold to raise the required $35,000 to build *Bluenose*, double the cost of any fishing schooner to that date.

BLUENOSE REGAINS THE CHAMPION'S MANTLE

TOP RIGHT

In 1921, the American entry to defend the Halifax Herald's International Fishermen's Trophy was *Mayflower*, pictured here. Although she had accomplished the mandatory fishing season on the Grand Banks, the Board of Trustees responsible for enforcing the rules disqualified *Mayflower* on the grounds that her design characteristics classed her "primarily a racing rather than a fishing vessel, and this contravened the conditions provided under the 'Deed of Gift'." The Americans were fit to be tied, claiming that the Lunenburgers were afraid of losing to her. Back and forth the bantering went but the decision stood. The disqualification of *Mayflower* prevented what may have been the greatest race that never was. Angus Walters regretted never having the chance to face her. "The Committee was scared of us racing the *Mayflower*," he was to say later, "though I would have been quite happy to do so. I had a good look at her on the marine railway once, and I knew then she'd be no trouble for us. I told them so, but they stuck to their guns." Following *Bluenose*'s fishing trip to the Grand Banks in April 1921 to qualify for the elimination heats, she returned to Halifax and easily defeated nine other vessels vying to represent Canada. She then cast aside the American's late replacement *Elsie* (captained by Marty Welsh) in similar fashion, beating her in two straight races around the Halifax course, first by thirteen minutes, then coming from far back in a race closer than the time would indicate to win the second by eleven minutes.

AMERICAN CHALLENGER *MAYFLOWER*

**BLUENOSE
VICTORIOUS
IN FIRST
DEFENSE OF
INTERNATIONAL
TITLE**

In 1922, *Bluenose* again defeated all comers at home, then sailed to Gloucester in defense of her title against the newly built challenger *Henry Ford* featured in this photo. Sporting the champion's '#1' on her sail, *Bluenose* had a harder time of it on this occasion. She lost the first race but it was declared unofficial to the chagrin of both captains because of false starts by the two vessels. *Bluenose* then lost the next one before storming back to take the last two and retain the title. In response to some who offered the excuse *Henry Ford* had lost the match because her fore-topmast had been carried away in strong winds during the second official race, Angus Walters replied with his usual wry humor: "Well, I'll tell you. I never wore no coat or oilskins and if there was any spray flyin' I never felt it. 'Course there was some water around, where we was sloshin' her down to keep her cool on the deck. Certainly not the kind of weather you look for a topmast to go in. Leastways, ours didn't."

**BLUENOSE
CREW AND
WELL-
WISHERS
POSE WITH
HALIFAX
HERALD
TROPHY**

There were two crews who manned the *Bluenose*. One was the usual fishing crew who sailed her to the Grand Banks. The other was a hand-picked, by invitation-only, racing crew for the International Fishermen's competition. Fishing or racing, the only skipper to ever take *Bluenose*'s helm was Capt. Angus Walters (pictured with hand on hip). Brian and Phil Backman in their book *Bluenose* offered a light-hearted account of an incident that followed the fabled fishing schooner's inaugural 1921 victory:

> The rejoicing in Halifax and along the coast that autumn night can well be imagined. Aboard *Bluenose*, a joyful crewman did a jig, proposed they all "tie one on" and begged "the borry of a chaw" off a fellow crew member-all in one breath. "Great jumpin' codfish, Bingie," growled his exasperated shipmate, "don't you ever buy any?" Then, resigning himself to the inevitable, he dug a huge ham of a hand down through dripping oilskins, bent double, plumbed the depths of an inner pocket and rummaged searchingly about in the region of his crotch. Finally, he straightened and brought forth a virgin plug of the dank, dark chewing tobacco so beloved of the saltbank fisherman. A moment later he got it back from the pan-handler and gazed ruefully at the bit that remained. "Bingie," he cautioned, "You'll likely find det a leedle damp this mornin'. I don't hold my vater like I used tuh."

CONTROVERSY MARRED 1923 RACE

While the salt bankers may have staged friendly races among themselves on their homeward voyages from the Grand Banks, the International Fishermen's Races were all business and often marred by controversy. A case in point was the 1923 race. As expected, *Bluenose* sailed from her homeport of Lunenburg to Halifax in defense of her crown where the American challenger *Columbia*, whose crew is featured in this photo, awaited her. Having easily defeated the *Henry Ford* in qualifiers, it was claimed that the *Columbia* personified "the very essence of speed itself." During the first heat, *Bluenose* and *Columbia* raced neck and neck, so close in fact that at the Third Buoy *Bluenose* chanced ramming *Columbia* to avoid wrecking on the "Three Sisters" ledge, while her opponent held course on the inside. Their sails and rigging became briefly entangled with *Bluenose* towing the challenger for nearly a minute before breaking away to win by two minutes. Surprisingly, no protests were lodged but the race rules were amended there and then to cover similar occurrences in the future. *Bluenose* took the second race as well by nearly three minutes but was disqualified under the newly implemented rules for passing a buoy on the wrong side. Despite Capt. Walters argument that the buoy in question was a channel and not a distance marker and, therefore, not part of the course, the decision stood and the contest was tied at one each. Walters was outraged and sailed *Bluenose* home to Lunenburg. *Columbia* meanwhile refused to sail the course alone to claim victory and the International Fishermen's Race of 1923 ended in a no contest. It would be seven years before another was held.

OLD FOES Lunenburg's Capt. Angus Walters (left) and Capt. Ben Pine, a native Newfoundlander who moved to Gloucester in 1893 at the age of ten and began dory haddock fishing, were long-time friends and three-time opponents in the International Fishermen's Races. Both were legendary skippers and respected sportsmen. In 1921, when *Bluenose* reclaimed the Halifax Trophy, Walters had slowed his vessel to make it a fair race in one heat after the American challenger *Elsie* had lost her fore-topmast. Pine had refused to sail the *Columbia* around the Halifax course uncontested to claim victory in 1923 when Walters withdrew *Bluenose* in protest.

Born at Lunenburg in 1882, taken to sea at age thirteen by his father, and a doryman at the age of fifteen, the stories of Angus Walters' skills at the helm, and as a leader of men, in times of fishing, racing, and storms are legion. For all the fame and achievements, however, he was by accounts a humble man, his life's ambition best summed up in his own words: "I never wanted to be better than any other man. I always wanted to be just as good."

INTER-
NATIONAL
FISHERMEN'S
RACE
REVIVED IN
1931

In 1930, *Bluenose* sailed to Gloucester in response to an invitation to race against the American schooner *Gertrude L. Thebaud*, pictured here, for the Sir Thomas Lipton Cup. Captained by Ben Pine the recently completed vessel defeated a sluggish *Bluenose* winning the final and deciding heat in the best of three race. Buoyed by their victory, the Americans clamored for a return engagement to decide the Halifax Herald's International Fishermen's champion. They got their wish the following year. The two vessels squared off at Halifax in October 1931, the *Gertrude L. Thebaud* beating the *Elsie* for American honors, the *Bluenose* representing Canada by acclamation. Considered old at ten years and water-logged from many seasons on the Grand Banks, *Bluenose* rose to the challenge of her much younger adversary. The first race was easily won by the aging Queen but it was thrown out because light winds had prevented completion of the course in the required six hours. Such was not the case in the next two; *Bluenose* won both to remain the undisputed champion of international racing.

Following another hiatus of seven years, *Bluenose* sailed to Gloucester in 1938 for one final defense of her title. Waiting as expected was the *Gertrude L. Thebaud* with Ben Pine at her helm. *Bluenose* was now well into her twilight years as were the international races. The days of sail were long past (*Bluenose* had diesel motors installed in 1936) and this would be the finale for the International Fishermen's Races. In a desperate attempt to wrestle the crown away, the Americans had managed to lengthen the races to a best of five affair. It mattered little. Having relied on one another for seventeen years in many a precarious moment, Walters and *Bluenose* bonded as one for the last time and retained the Halifax Trophy in a closely fought five-race match. Basking in glory, the two warriors sailed home to Lunenburg, leaving the Americans with only Walter's long-time prophecy ringing in their ears: "The wood of the vessel that will beat the *Bluenose* is still growing."

BLUENOSE DIED A PAUPER

As a working vessel *Bluenose* was highliner of the Lunenburg Grand Banks fleet. As a racer, she never tasted defeat at the International Fishermen's Races. Her likeness adorned a fifty-cent stamp in 1929 and was pressed onto the Canadian ten-cent piece in 1937. She represented the Maritimes at the 1933 Chicago World's Fair and sailed to England in 1935 as the nation's ambassador for the Silver Jubliee of King George V and Queen Mary. Despite all this, she died a pauper. Having returned to Lunenburg from her 1938 victory in Gloucester, *Bluenose* was in debt, her fishing days behind her. Lost in the storm clouds of World War Two, even Angus Walters putting up seven thousand dollars of his own money could not save the grand old lady and in 1942 she was sold to the West Indian Trading Company. Shorn of her towering Oregon pine masts, *Bluenose* finished her days as a tramp in the Caribbean coastal trade, finally coming to grief far from home one January night in 1946 on a reef off Haiti. Two years later, the *Gertrude L. Thebaud* joined her, sinking after striking a breakwater in the port of La Guadera, Venezuela.

Ironically, none of the vessels that contested for the Halifax Trophy "died in bed of old age."

Esperanto went down off Sable Island and *Columbia* foundered there in the Gale of 1927, taking her twenty-two-man Nova Scotia crew with her. *Henry Ford* sank off Martin Point, Newfoundland a year later and the *Elsie* followed in 1935 near St. Pierre. Even *Mayflower* didn't survive. A footnote to the saga was carried in the March 28, 1999 *Halifax Sunday Herald*, which stated that divers believed they have located *Bluenose*'s final resting place and hope to at least salvage her anchor from the more than twenty that litter the site.

Chapter 7

Leisure, Customs, & Special Events

FISHERMEN'S PICNIC

The first fishermen's picnic on record to be held in Lunenburg County was staged at Ritcey's Cove on September 21, 1887 in aid of widow Peeler; sixty dollars was raised. The town of Lunenburg held its inaugural festivities in 1916, featured in this postcard portrayal, as a re-union for fishermen "after their arduous labor on the fishing grounds." Amid much pomp and circumstance, six hundred school children led a 'Trades Procession' of floats and marching bands along Lincoln Street followed by speeches from town fathers and local politicians. The afternoon was taken up with a variety of challenge matches including a fat man's race for men 190 pounds and over, and tug-of-war pulls between fishermen and shoremen from Lunenburg and Riverport. The evening was capped off with band concerts and a fire works display. A newspaper account proclaimed the picnic a resounding success and "so much interest was taken in the affair, and so thorough a day's sports was held that the affair will be made an annual one." The Fishermen's Picnic did indeed become a yearly autumn attraction, evolving into Nova Scotia's first Fisheries Exhibition in 1929, and attracting eleven thousand people in 1931 to the then three-day event.

DORY RACES, FISHERMEN'S PICNIC, 1916

For the thousands of spectators who came to Lunenburg in September, 1916 for the Fishermen's Picnic, a main attraction was the dory races staged on the waterfront. Although the event was no doubt initially held between fishermen from various vessels for local bragging rights, the dory races eventually turned into an international competition. The greatest dory racers to come out of Lunenburg were considered to be the team of Lloyd Heisler and Russell Langille who, in 1982, were inducted into the Nova Scotia Sports Hall of Fame. Lloyd Heisler who passed away in 1997 at the age of ninety-one, was a crew member of the original *Bluenose* and began double-dory racing in the 1920s at the Lunenburg Fishermen's Picnics. Heisler and Langille became legendary, winning twenty-seven races over the course of twenty-one years. In 1952 Gloucester, Massachusetts issued a challenge to Lunenburg for a dory race which Heisler-Langille "won hands-down." They captured six international titles, three at Gloucester and three at Lunenburg, before hanging up their oars in 1955. Interestingly, one of Lloyd Heisler's early partners was Adam Selig whose name appears as a first place winner in the double-dory race of 1916.

SPECIAL OCCASIONS

TOP RIGHT

A Lunenburg Foundry float passes under one of two evergreen arches erected along Lunenburg's Lincoln Street in celebration of Queen Victoria's 1897 Diamond Jubilee. The 1800s were a time when much attention was paid to civic celebrations in honour of special occasions and visiting dignitaries. Queen Victoria's coronation in 1837, the centenary of Lunenburg's founding in 1853, the marriage of Prince of Wales in 1863, and Canada's Confederation in 1867 were just some of the events for which Lunenburgers fired royal salutes, rang bells, hung great displays of flags and bunting, organized elaborate parades through the streets, held athletic competitions, and staged "grand illuminations" of fireworks.

SPECIAL OCCASIONS

LUNENBURG CYCLISTS
A growing interest in sports during the late 1800s led to the establishment of a Lunenburg YMCA in 1890 and the Lunenburg Amateur Athletic Association. The Lunenburg A.A.A. sponsored a bicycle race in 1896 with Thomas Naas setting a provincial record in the three-mile race and a Maritime record for the five-miler. At this time Lunenburg also had Nova Scotia's finest bicycle race track.

VAUDEVILLIAN BILLY KING

Lunenburg native Billy King, shown here flanked by his brothers, learned to ride a unicycle at the age of fifteen. Taught by other performers, and perfecting his own routines, King went on to the life of a vaudevillian-juggling, chair and table balancing, hoop spinning, and performing bicycle stunts. He worked for Neil Brothers Circus in Montreal and the Hollywood Daredevils. In his later years, he remained a popular attraction in local exhibitions and fairs.

HOCKEY WAS ONE OF MANY ATTRACT-IONS AT THE DRILL SHED

TOP RIGHT

Rupert Kaulbach is credited with introducing hockey to Lunenburg in 1898 after having seen it played in Upper Canada while attending college there. The original Lunenburg Victoria team could have possibly played some of its early home games in the Drill Shed, a training centre for local militia groups that was framed at Boston in 1840 from local private funds, then shipped in pieces and reconstructed at Lunenburg. Over the years, the Drill Shed became the centre for many community attractions including skating, vaudeville acts, theatre groups, church bazaars, band concerts, county exhibitions, and a prize fight featuring the legendary John L. Sullivan. On one occasion, a professional walker came to town, challenging all comers to a heel-toe race. Local sportsman John Nauss easily defeated him on a circuitous route around the building.

In 1902, the Drill Shed, which still stands today under town management, was taken over by the federal Department of Militia and Defence, later re-named the Lunenburg Armouries, and for many years after served as a recruiting and training facility. The most noted unit to come out of Lunenburg was the 75th Lunenburg Regiment whose members served with distinction in the Great War and in 1936 were amalgamated into the much-heralded West Nova Scotia Regiment of World War Two.

VICTORIA
HOCKEY TEAM
LUNENBURG N.S.

HOCKEY WAS ONE OF MANY ATTRACTIONS AT THE DRILL SHED

**CANNON
GATE PARK**
Mather DesBrisay offers a description of the fine view of the town and its surrounding from atop "The Sherriff's head, now known as Kaulbach Head and the site of a golf course:

> On it is a large piece of forest called Cannon Park, the property of C.E. Kaulbach, Esq., M.P., by whom it is generously loaned for picnics and public purposes. Two large cannon are placed at the entrance gate, and two others are mounted at the edge of the woods. In the grove is an arch formed of large bones of a whale. There is a good foot-road through the park to the shore. Much money has been spent by the owner on the park property and the adjoining land.

Used extensively for picnics and various gatherings and special events, much of Sheriff's Head in the 1930s was turned into the present-day Bluenose Golf Course.

LUNENBURG WAS NOTED FOR MUSIC

An undated photo of an early Salvation Army band. The first band of note was the Artillery Band formed in the 1830s, possibly for Queen Victoria's 1837 coronation festivities. By 1895 there were seven "fully equipped" brass bands in the county, Lunenburg and Mahone Bay having two each, with one at Bridgewater, Ritcey's Cove and Petite Riviere respectively. German residents, in particular, were noted for their singing prowess. A Bach amateur orchestra was organized and trained by the Reverend Albert R.J Graepp at Bridgewater which "with its musical talent, bids fair to win popular applause." Calvin Wheelock, while living in Bridgewater, taught music in Lunenburg during the 1830s at what was reputedly the first regular singing school in the county.

75TH BATTALLION BAND

TOP RIGHT

The most famous of the Lunenburg bands was the 75th Volunteers Battallion Band. According to historian Brian Cuthbertson, the band performed on every civic occasion....As the result of their outstanding musicianship at the 1909 Dominion Exhibition in Halifax, the band was selected to play at the Boston Mechanics Exhibition. There, a critic who had heard all the best bands for years at the Exhibition and also the Coldstream Guards and the Black Watch, supposed to be the finest in the world, declared he "had never heard any band to produce the music that took such a hold on the people as the 75th Regiment Band of Lunenburg, Nova Scotia."

The band members are: back row, left to right: Al English, C. Zinck, C. Backman, W. Langille, George Townshend, Clarence Jeffery, R. Naas, Bob Berringer, Chas. Jeffery, Bandmaster, John Arenburg, A. Hebb, Jas. Anderson, Fred Morgan, Wm. Townshend, front row, left-right: Albert Anderson, H.H. Anderson, R. Beck, Sam Mack, Wm. Heisler.

75TH BATTALLION BAND

MODEL BOATS

Featured in this early 1900s photo is thought to be the interior of a boating clubhouse at Lunenburg. The model schooners were sailed in mini-regattas along the harbour shore. DesBrisay makes several references in his county history to the popularity of making and sailing model boats. At the Industrial Exhibition held at Chester in 1889, a model schooner measuring four feet in length, built by Hibbert Richard from Park's Creek, was "one of the leading attractions...and has been pronounced an almost perfect model by many of our skippers."

In 1892, Lunenburg's William Heisler was noted for building a miniature of the steamboat Lunenburg and he "intends, if the weather proves favorable, to try the boat on Lunenburg Harbor in a fortnight's time." The same year, the *Hants Journal* published a detailed account of a model steamship, the Windsor, built at Lunenburg by James E. Rafuse, "on which he has been at work for about a year past, mainly in the evenings." Perhaps Lunenburg's most noted early model builder was also one of its best shipwrights, Stephen Morash, who entered a number of his in various competitions. In 1881 he won a prize of thirty dollars for a miniature fishing boat and schooner at Halifax and again in 1884 and 1894 he was awarded medals for a brigantine, schooner, and canoe.

NOVA SCOTIA GUIDES MEET, LAKE WILLIAM CA. 1930

In 1909 a small group of woodsmen met at South Milford, Annapolis County to form the Nova Scotia Guides Association. At that time they held a one-day competition featuring six events that included canoe racing, log rolling, chopping, shooting, swimming, and fly-casting. Over the years, the meets became an annual attraction when the guides got together to discuss game laws and conservation issues affecting their profession. The meets peaked during the 1930s when held at Lake William, Lunenburg County. More than one hundred and thirty guides competed then in forty events over the course of one week held during the full moon of August. The Nova Scotia Guides Meet made headline news in the daily papers, was covered on radio and became the social event of the summer, attracting daily crowds of ten to fifteen thousand people, from as far away as the United States, Quebec, and Ontario.

FUNERALS

In 1896 there were two undertakers plying their trade in Lunenburg; Eli Hopps on Montague Street and Joseph Spencer on Lincoln Street. The automobiles in this photo indicate an early 1900s ceremony. Mather DesBrisay writes in his 1895 county history of earlier rites and rituals:

> Sorrowful seasons were observed in a manner differing from present practice. The dead were carried some distance for interment at Lunenburg and the funeral procession was met by friends, at or near the entrance to the town, from whence to the grave singers preceded the corpse, and in sweetly appropriate German hymns gave expression to the general feeling of grief for the loss of the departed. In this county the procession was often halted, and hymns were sung at different places on the way to the churchyard.
>
> When children were buried, artificial flowers were made by the girls, which, being fastened round hoops, and otherwise arranged, were carried in the procession; and, after the interment of the body, were laid on the grave, stones being placed on them to keep them from being blown away.

FUNERAL PROCESSION

Featured here are members of the Right Worthy Grand Orange Lodge of Nova Scotia which formed its Lunenburg chapter in 1858.

Since both of these photos were encased in the same frame it would indicate the lines of Orangemen await arrival of the funeral procession bearing one of their recently departed members.

BAPTISMS AND WEDDINGS WERE TIMES TO FEAST AND DANCE

A ca. 1905 photo of an unidentified infant and lady. The clothes indicate some special occasion, perhaps a baptism or christening. At this time, these events were infused with festivity and open rejoicing, as family and friends would spend the entire day following the ritual at a party at the home of the child's parents.

Weddings encouraged even more celebration. Following the exchange of church vows, guests retired to the nearest tavern and "partook of refreshments" before heading to the main party, where a fiddler was kept busy, sometimes for days, entertaining the revellers in "dancing and other amusements." It was customary for the bride's shoe to be passed to each guest for a cash donation or to be auctioned, the proceeds then returned to the bride. A tradition in later years was for each guest to donate one dollar.

Wedding feasts were known to involve twenty to twenty-five gallons of spirits and several sheep, geese and pigs laid out with a variety of soups, pies, cakes and puddings. A wash tub was commonly used to mix an old recipe requiring twelve dozen eggs for the wedding cake. Guests were considered rude should they leave before everything was eaten. One Bridgewater resident is said to have attended five of these "protracted wedding-feasts" in one autumn.

TALISMANS   This photo is of special interest for several reasons. Note the horse-shoe on the parlor door in the background. According to tradition, this was hung improperly. To catch and hold in good luck the heel should have been inverted. Such beliefs were indicative of the numerous superstitions held by many of the original settlers who often attached great significance to omens, charms, and witchcraft.

Another interesting feature of the photo is the people portrayed. Although unidentified, the photo comes from the Bailly Family collection at the provincial archives and may very well be Edwin Bailly, a well-known Lunenburg blacksmith at the turn-of-the-century, and his family. The Bailly name dates to the founding of Lunenburg when "the first birth in the new community was that of Jane Margaret Bailly, which occurred during the night following the landing, in a rude camp built among the bushes."

A unique photo of an early Lunenburg Christmas tree. Close inspection reveals
candles among the many decorations and what appears to be a Santa Claus near
the tree top flanked by small flags. A number of Christmas traditions can be
traced to Germany including Advent wreaths and calendars. The custom of
putting up a Christmas tree has been attributed to Martin Luther, founder of
the Lutheran Church, who first set an evergreen in his children's nursery to mark
the night of Christ's birth. Decorations were a later feature which early German settlers introduced to the colonies. However, it was not until Queen Victoria married
Prince Albert, a German, that decorated Christmas trees became widely popular.
Sometime in the 1840s, Albert put a tree up one Christmas Eve for the Queen
and their children. A photo marking the event later appeared in newspapers around
the world and a Christmas tradition was born.

Chapter 8

County Life

LUNENBURG WOMEN WORKED HARD ON THE FARMS

Fishing was not a lucrative profession for most men who crewed the salt bankers; even in the early 1900s, an annual average salary was still less than two hundred dollars. To survive, most worked farms to feed their families and grow produce that could be sold for outfitting the Lunenburg fleet. The historian DesBrisay noted that, "Hundreds of the men of the county, owners of small farms, are absent in the summer at deep-sea fishing. During their absence the women employ themselves hoeing potatoes and doing other farm work. This they supplement by the assistance they give on the return of the fishermen in spreading the fish for 'making.' It cannot be said that out-door work does not agree with them so far as health is concerned, for they are very strong and fresh-looking." In this photo, thought to be taken in Lunenburg County, five women rake hay into stacks while a sixth lady rides a horse-drawn mower. It has been said that, "next to the oxen, the women probably worked the hardest, the average lifetime career of a fisherman's wife being to 'split fish and bear children.'"

A FARMER'S LIFE

Within a year of Lunenburg's founding, one hundred families had moved from the town to live on their farm lots. Over the next century, settlement along the coast and the interior expanded, based in large measure on farming. By the late 1800s, Conquerall, Campertown, Lapland, Baker Settlement, Waterloo, Chelsea, Midville Branch, Lower Branch, Northfield, Riversdale, Foster Settlement, and New Germany were all noted farming communities. In 1891, New Germany was "one of the most thriving agricultural districts in the county" and with 3,838 residents it had the fourth largest population behind Lunenburg with 4,894 people, Block House with a population of 4,153, and Bridgewater with 3,936. The predominant crops grown in the county were potatoes, apples, cabbages, turnips, barley, oats, rye, and hay. Lunenburg apples were considered "almost equal" to those of the more famous Annapolis Valley. Cabbage, a staple food item particularly amongst people of German descent, was especially plentiful, often growing impressive sizes. In November 1894, Mr. Sylvester Baker, of Big Tancook Island, pulled two cabbages from his field, one of which weighed 25 1/2 pounds, and the other 23 1/2 pounds. District agricultural societies were organized as early as 1819 and the first provincial exhibition was held at Halifax in 1854. In 1882, a John Anderson entered strawberries five inches in circumference at a town fair, while in 1895, Daniel Rudolph displayed gooseberries measuring three-and-a-half inches.

EARLY FERRIES

TOP RIGHT

Lorenzo Parks, featured here rowing a lady passenger with her carriage and horse across the LaHave, was one of several ferry operators on the river in the 1800s. At Lower Dublin was Himmelman's Ferry and at Glen Allan was James Nicholson's scow ferry. The first ferry in the county is attributed to a man by the name of Kolp who began his business in the mid-1700s between South (now Bayport) and Lunenburg. The distance was about three miles and the fare charged was four pennies for a return ticket. The story goes that on one occasion, Kolp was forced to part with his red cap, which was sent into the harbor by the wind of a cannon ball, which passed unpleasantly close to his head.

A NINETEENTH-CENTURY FERRY

GOLD MINING AT THE OVENS

Mining was never a major industry in Lunenburg County but gold discoveries at the Ovens, Gold River, Chester Basin, Millipsigit, and Vogler's Cove in the mid-nineteenth century caused the usual excitement that accompanies such finds. The Ovens are steep cliffs containing deep caverns worn into the sides by wave action from storms and high tides. A gold rush of sorts "imparted a stimulus to the prosperity of Lunenburg" in 1861-62 when the precious metal was found along the bluff at the Ovens. Most claims, some selling for $4800, concentrated on the beach below the cliffs; of the 1,282 ounces found between 1861-1864, one thousand were panned from alluvial washings in 1861-62 as pictured here.

Being only four miles by water from Lunenburg the town was abuzz: "Whole talk is gold, gold, gold. Excitement intense." Dry goods merchant Adolphus Gaetz's journal spanning the years 1855-1873, contained many entries about the affect of this development on Lunenburg and the surrounding area in 1861:

July 16th About one hundred gold-hunters arrived.

July 22nd Ovens attracting attention of whole Province.

August 6th Steamer Osprey arrived, with workmen, lumber, etc.

August 8th Town full of strangers. Hotels full. Some had to pitch their tents on the common.

August 10th Steamer Neptune arrived with seventy-five passengers. Packet from Halifax, with 104 additional.

August 31st Upwards of six hundred now at work. Shanties erected, and grocery shops and restaurants opened.

Prospecting went on for a number of years at the Ovens but no one came away wealthy. It was estimated each miner averaged only slightly more than one ounce per month worked.

Oak Island, Chester Bay, where Capt. Kidd buried his Gold

TREASURE HUNTING

In the summer of 1795, sixteen-year-old Daniel McGinnis of Chester rowed his boat to nearby Oak Island. While roaming the island, he came upon ring bolts in rocks, moss covered stumps, grown over pathways, and a tackle-block hanging from the limb of an ancient oak tree in a clearing. With visions of treasure and privateers he returned the following day with two friends, John Smith and Anthony Vaughan, to look unsuccessfully for plunder. Thus began one of the world's greatest treasure hunts. While many have tried, including the likes of Franklin Roosevelt and John Wayne, Oak Island has refused to divulge her secrets. Speculation as to what is buried there has run the gamut including Captain Kidd's treasure, or Sir Francis Drake's booty, plundered from Spanish ships in the Caribbean. Some believe the "money pit" may be a communal pirate bank while others lean towards it housing a vault built by French or British colonial authorities. Even the Shakespearean manuscripts of Francis Bacon and the lost treasure of Tumbez, Peru have been linked to Oak Island. Without question something is, or was, buried there. Lives have been lost and millions of dollars invested trying to unravel this puzzle which continues to mystify after more than two hundred years.

BRIDGEWATER WHARVES, LATE 1800S

Here, vessels are loading lumber at Bridgewater, the "chief place of business on the LaHave River." As early as the 1860s, Lunenburg County was the largest producer of spruce and hemlock boards in the province. By 1871, there were 1,144 sawmills in Nova Scotia, 1,126 being water-powered. Of these, the four largest were on the LaHave River at or near Bridgewater. Two were owned and operated by E.D. Davison & Sons which employed 114 men and produced 7,800,000 board feet of lumber annually. S.P. Benjamin owned the other two mills with sixty employees and a yearly production of 5,500,000 board feet.

For three miles below Bridgewater, the LaHave River was too narrow to be navigated by vessels under sail. At one time, three ships would be towed together through this stretch of river by as many as five yoke of oxen. A towage fee of one to two dollars was charged for a schooner, more for larger vessels. One man walking along the river bank one hundred feet from the teams was responsible for keeping the towing ropes clear of rocks. Oxen were replaced in 1869 by the steam tug *Gypsy*, pictured here, and in 1871 by the tug *La Have*. E.D. Davison & Sons was sold to American interests in 1902 and renamed Davison Lumber Co. Ltd. By January 1, 1906, ninety vessels were under charter to the company, all loading out of Bridgewater.

SHIP TIMBER FOR LUNENBURG

The caption for this photo reads "Archie Hebb (L) and J. Harold Hebb (R) with loads of ship timber for Lunenburg, N.S. 1904. Picture taken in front of railway station, Bridgewater. Timber from Oak Hill Farm, Wileville." An interesting feature are the timbers themselves which have been cut from stumps with large roots dug from the ground and sawn off in varying lengths. These were then shaped by shipwrights at the yards into 'knees' which served as braces at angled junctures in a vessel's construction, that is where a deck and the side of the hull met. Larch or tamarack were generally chosen for knees but in very large ships they could be cut from split sections of oak or yellow birch where a branch and trunk intersected. Red oak was preferred early on for ship timbers but yellow birch was eventually found to be superior in its resistance to rot from continual soaking.

MAHONE BAY AND CHESTER WERE SHIPBUILDING CENTRES

TOP RIGHT

Lunenburg County had many shipyards building vessels for the fishing and mercantile trade. Mahone Bay, pictured here with a ship on the stocks, featured several builders of note-Titus Langille, Stephen Langille, John H. Zwicker, Elkanah Zwicker, D.E. Burgoyne, Isiah Wagner, McLeod & Copeland, J. Ernst & Sons, and John McLean who started McLean Construction Co. in the 1850s when he moved to Mahone Bay from Shelburne. More than three hundred vessels, some in excess of four hundred tons were built at Mahone Bay.

A short distance to the east at Chester Basin were the yards of I. Wagner and the Chester Shipbuilding Co. The town of Chester also had several shipyards, the best known being the Standford Boat Building Co., Joseph C. Morgan, Charles Walther, and William Marvin, who, before his death in 1872, built more than 350 vessels. Charles Hilchey built 300 at Chester prior to 1877, and was followed in the trade by his son Samuel who repaired 1000 boats of various kinds and launched 100 of his own.

SHIPBUILDING AT MAHONE BAY

LAHAVE RIVER SHIPBUILDING

The LaHave River, featured here ca. 1895, was a major centre of ship building activity until the early 1920s. Vessels in a variety of sizes and designs were built for local lumber and fish merchants as well as many contracted by Newfoundland interests involved in the fish trade. Canada's first three-masted schooner, or 'tern' as they were called, was the *Zebra*, built in 1859 at LaHave. J.N. Rafuse of Conquerall Bank built many schooners as did Albert McKean at Pleasantville, Melbourne Leary at Dayspring and Fred Robar on the LaHave River.

James Weagle, his son George and grandson Jacob built more than forty schooners at Summerside as did Stephen Leary. A number of vessels were also launched in other communities along the shore-at Petite Riviere, West Dublin, Broad Cove, and Vogler's Cove.

J.N. Rafuse & Sons Shipyard, Conquerall Bank

Depending upon the size of the yard it generally took four or five months to build a schooner, then a few more weeks to rig her for sailing.

In his *Sails of the Maritimes*, John P. Parker describes what was needed to build the boats:

> In the small shipyards scattered around the coast the prime requisites were a sheltered beach with an ample depth of water at high tide to float a sizable vessel, together with a sufficient supply of suitable timber within easy hauling distance from the yard...A steam plant was required to run the big saw, the planers and for heat in the steam-box where planks could be "softened up" for bending. Apart from the steam plant, a few teams of horses or oxen, a blacksmith's forge and a covered floor for laying off lines, there was little else required than individual carpenter tools.

CHESTER

**CHESTER-
"BAR
HARBOUR OF
NOVA
SCOTIA"**

BOTTOM LEFT

In August, 1759 Nova Scotia was divided into five counties, Lunenburg being one. The county was then sub-divided into three townships—Lunenburg, New Dublin, and Shoreham, later changed to Chester. The town of Chester itself was established in August 1759 by settlers from Boston and around the mid-1800s it had become a popular summer destination. On September 4, 1856 Chester hosted the county's first regatta. Still a celebrated holiday location today, the town provided plenty of allure in the nineteenth century as this passage from DesBrisay's 1895 *History of Lunenburg County* attests:

> Chester has long been a favorite resort for United States tourists, and has proved attractive to many from the interior of this Province and other parts of Canada. It has a remarkably fine harbor, of sufficient depth for large vessels. The hotel accommodation is pronounced to be very good, and there are excellent facilities for sea bathing and boating, with good fishing and smooth roads for carriage driving. It ought to be more largely visited by those in search of health or pleasure.

> One of the town's interesting character's of the time was Chester native Capt. James Pattillo (1807-87) considered to be one of the strongest men "ever born on this continent." It was claimed "the grasp of his hand might almost crush the handle of an oar." One day on Mitchell's Wharf in Chester he was observed lifting barrels of pickled fish by only the chimes, or rim, from the hold of his vessel onto the deck. He was then able to "support one of the barrels on one of his broad shoulders, and then lift it backwards over his head, and lay it on his neck and shoulders. Having had them properly placed, he carried a barrel of the fish on each shoulder into Mitchell's store."

MI'KMAQ CAMP NEAR CHESTER, CA. 1910

In 1861 there were only thirty-eight Mi'kmaq still living in Lunenburg County, their people having been decimated in large part by small pox. By 1891 the numbers had increased only marginally to fifty-nine. No longer "robust and energetic" and considered "much neglected," the native Mi'kmaq were described as living generally in "a rudely constructed hut, or small house, close to a town or village, (where) he makes axe-handles, mast-hoops, and other articles of woodenware, in which work he shows much neatness and skill, leading a life in a great degree incompatible with the desires natural to his race."

Dry cod being loaded onto the schooner *Mauna Loa* from an ox-drawn sleigh on the ice in Lunenburg Harbour, 1905. Oxen were once synonymous with Lunenburg County. In 1767, there were 218 oxen and bulls in the township and only forty-four horses. The 1891 Census lists 5,050 working oxen compared to only 1,213 horses. Oxen were less expensive to feed than horses (they could be turned loose and left to graze on meadow grass in summer), and they were better adapted to working on rocky ground or swampy terrain. Early accounts make frequent reference to the poor condition of roads, passable only with ox-drawn sleds. Even when winter snows reached extremes, building up to over four feet on the level in the woods, oxen were reported to have "travelled without difficulty."

TOP RIGHT

A team of oxen pose with their teamster and wagon-load of dunnage, ca. 1900. Oxen were multi-purpose animals, capable of clearing, tilling, and plowing farmland, harvesting crops, making hay, dragging logs from the woods, hauling freight, and then supplying leather and beef at the end of their working lives. A classic example of the oxen's usefulness was illustrated in the early 1800s when Frederick Hiltz built the schooner *James William* at Clearland, about three-quarters of a mile from Mahone Bay: "Thirty-six pairs of oxen were attached to a sled constructed for the purpose, and the vessel was thus conveyed to the salt water."

OXEN TEAM

SNOW STORMS

In his *Images of Lunenburg*, Peter Barss quotes an elderly Lunenburg resident reflecting on how the area was affected by snowstorms during his boyhood:

> Sometimes it would take you, I'd say as high as t'ree days to get the roads open after a big snowstorm. There was no snowploughs. We was the ploughs! Everyt'in was done wit' a shovel. In the fall of the year, you see, you were sworn in as a road overseer. Now, on a big snowstorm you had to get out an' you had your district to go in-perhaps a mile'd be your section. An' everybody that lives on that section, you'd come to the house say at nine o'clock for shovellin' snow. An' then, from there on, the next overseer'd would warn his men out an' that's the way you'd get the roads open...

EVERYBODY SEEMED SO HAPPY
Two photos depicting the "simple life" of an earlier era. One features a typical country store near Mahone Bay which not only housed all the necessary staples from groceries and dry goods to seeds and feed but also served as a community meeting place to catch up on the most recent news and gossip. The other shows that not everyone lived in stately Victorian style homes built from the fruits of the fishery.

"I always say people in them times was a lot happier than they are today," recalls a veteran fisherman in Peter Barss' *Images of Lunenburg County.*

> Sure. They didn't have so much...they didn't have what the people have today, but they didn't look for it either. You couldn't get the t'ings if they would'a been available. There wasn't as much money, but everybody seemed so happy. People did t'ings an' lived different an' mixed wit' one anot'er an' everybody was good friends. And now the world's divided like. There don't seem to be the same kind o' friends. Too much money. One person don't care for t'other. I remember back...there was nice feelin's in them times.

Sources

Armour, Charles & Lackey, Thomas. *Sailing Ships of the Maritimes.* Toronto: McGraw-Hill Ryerson Ltd., 1975.

Backman, Brian & Phil. *Bluenose.* Toronto: McClelland & Stewart, 1965.

Balcom, B.A. *History of the Lunenburg Fishing Industry.* Lunenburg: Lunenburg Marine Museum Society, 1977.

Barrett, Wayne & Walker, David A. Small *Wooden Boats of the Atlantic.* Halifax: Nimbus Publishing Ltd. 1990.

Barss, Peter. Images of Lunenburg County. Toronto: McClelland & Stewart, 1978.

Bellerose, George. *Facing the Open Sea: The People of Big Tancook Island.* Halifax. Nimbus Publishing Ltd., 1995.

Corkum, Hugh. *On Both Sides of the Law.* Hantsport, N.S.: Lancelot Press, 1989.

Creighton, Helen. *Bluenose Magic: Popular Beliefs and Superstitions in Nova Scotia.* Toronto: McGraw-Hill Ryerson Ltd. 1968.

Cuthbertson, Brian. *Lunenburg: An Illustrated History.* Halifax: Formac, 1996.

Darrach, Claude. *Race to Fame: The Inside Story of the Bluenose.* Hantsport: Lancelot Press, 1985.

DesBrisay, Mather Byles. *History of the County of Lunenburg.* Belleville, Ont.: Mika Publishing Co., 1980.

Effective Publishing Ltd. *The Lunenburg Times.* Halifax. 1999.

Gillespie, G.J. *Bluenose Skipper.* Fredericton, N.B.: Brunswick Press, 1955.

James, Terry & Anderson, Frances. *In Praise of Oxen.* Halifax: Nimbus Publishing Ltd. 1992.

James, Terry & Plaskett, Bill. *Buildings of Old Lunenburg.* Halifax:

Nimbus Publishing Ltd., 1996.

Jenson, L.B. *Fishermen of Nova Scotia.* Halifax: Petheric Press, 1980.

_____. *Bluenose II: Saga of the Great Fishing Schooners.* Halifax: Nimbus Publishing Ltd. 1994.

Johnson, Ralph S. *Forests of Nova Scotia.* Halifax: Four East Publications, 1986.

Lunenburg Heritage Society. *A Walk Through Old Lunenburg.* Lunenburg, 1979.

McAlpine's Directory For The County of Lunenburg 1891, 1896, 1908. Halifax: McAlpine Publishing Co. Ltd.

McLaren, Keith R. *Bluenose & Bluenose II.* Willowdale, Ont.: Hounslow Press. 1981.

Pacey, Elizabeth & Comiter, Alvin. *Landmarks: Historic Buildings of Nova Scotia.* Halifax: Nimbus Publishing Ltd. 1994.

Parker, John P. *Sails of the Maritimes.* Aylesburg & Slough, Great Britain: Hazell Watson & Viney Ltd. 1960.

Plaskett, Bill. *Understanding Lunenburg's Architecture*. Lunenburg: Lunenburg Heritage Society. 1979.

Pullen, H.F. & Jenson, L.B. *Atlantic Schooners*. Fredericton: Brunswick Press. 1967.

Roue, Joan E. *A Spirit Deep Within: Naval Architect W.J. Roue and the Bluenose Story*. Hantsport: Lancelot Press. 1995.

Spicer, Stanley T. *Masters of Sail*. Halifax: Petheric Press Ltd. 1968.

Wallace, Frederick William. *Wooden Ships & Iron Men*. London: White Lion Publishers, 1973.

Wanzel, Grant. *Lunenburg: Memories, Buildings, Places, Events*. Halifax: School of Architecture, TUNS. 1989.

Withrow, Alfreda. *St. Margaret's Bay: A History*. Halifax. Four East Publications Ltd. 1985.

Ziner, Feenie. *Bluenose: Queen of the Grand Banks*. Halifax: Nimbus Publishing Ltd. 1970

PHOTO CREDITS

t = top   b = bottom   r = right   l = left

On the following pages, images are courtesy of the Fisheries Museum of the Atlantic:
v, viii, ix, x, 7 (t), 8, 9, 11, 13, 14, 15, 16, 33, 35, 37 (b), 38, 52, 53, 54, 78 (t), 80 (b), 85, 88, 89, 90 (l), 93, 94, 98, 99 (t), 101, 107 (t), 115 (t), 116 (t).

On the following pages, images are courtesy of the Public Archives of Nova Scotia:
Bailly Familly Collection: 12, 22, 25, 27 (t), 44 (b), 46, 63, 66, 102, 103, 104, 115 (b),
A. Silver Collection: 30 (b), 49 (b), 99 (b),
W.L. Bishop Collection: 41,
E.A. Bollinger Collection: 50, 51,
Edith Read Collection: 112 (b), 113
Lunenburg File: 2,

On the following pages, images are courtesy of the Maritime Museum of the Atlantic:
F.W. Wallace Collection: 4, 10 (b), 17, 18, 20, 36, 39, 67, 68, 69, 70, 71, 72, 73, 74, 77, 78 (b), 79, 81, 87 (b)
Miscellaneous Files: 1, 19, 37 (t), 42, 80 (t), 83, 84, 86, 87 (t), 90 (r), 110, 111 (b), 112 (t).

On the following pages, images are courtesy of the History Collection, Nova Scotia Museum, Halifax:
5 (75.34.9), 6 (92.33.61), 23 (t 87.111.10; b 87.111.11), 26 (t 87.111.20; b 78.30.4), 27 (b 87.111.12), 28 (b 87.111.12), 29 (P78.74), 30 (t P78.75), 32 (P135.69), 43 (92.33.56), 45 (t 87.128.1), 55 (87.111.17), 56 (87.111.14), 57 (72.18), 58 (P77.64), 59 (t 75.33.39; b P.129.68), 60 (87.111.16), 61 (87.111.90), 64 (P78.73), 65 (77.65.4), 95 (P78.72), 105 (87.111.51), 106 (87.111.32), 107 (b 80.7.2), 109 (P116.30), 111 (t 87.111.37), 116 (b 89.9.1).

On the following pages, images are courtesy of Knickles Studio & Gallery, Lunenburg: 3, 7 (b), 28 (t), 31, 34, 40 (t), 44 (t), 45 (b), 47, 48, 49 (t), 62, 75, 76, 95 (t), 114.

On the following pages, images are courtesy of Hugh Corkum, Lunenburg: 10 (t), 21, 24, 91, 92, 96, 97, 108.

On the following pages, images are from the author's personal collection:
40, 82, 100.

Photo on page 90 (l) is taken from the book *Bluenose*, by Brian and Phil Backman, Toronto: McClelland & Stewart, 1965.